Strategic Finan

Martin Potter,
Team Manager, PDSI Team,
Social Services Area Office,
Essington House,
Essington Way,
PETERLEE   SR8 5AZ

Strategic Financial Planning

for Public Sector Services

Strategic Financial Planning

for Public Sector Services

Essential skills for
The public sector

Jennifer Bean
Lascelles Hussey

Strategic Financial Planning for Public Sector Services

HB PUBLICATIONS
(Incorporated as Givegood Limited)

Published by:

**HB Publications
London, England**

British Library Cataloguing in Publication Data

ISBN 1899448128

© HB Publications (incorporated as Givegood Limited) 2000. All rights reserved; no part of this publication may be reproduced, stored in a mechanical retrieval system, or transmitted in any form or by any means, electronic, photocopying, recording, or otherwise, without either the prior written permsision of HB Publications or a licence permitting restricted copying issued by the Copyright Licensing Agency, 90 Tottenham Court Road, London W1T 4LP. This book may not be lent, resold, hired out or otherwise disposed of by way of trade in any form of binding or cover other than that in which it is published, without the prior consent of HB Publications.

Printed and bound in England by Short Run Press Ltd.

Contents

INTRODUCTION 1

FINANCIAL PLANNING 3
The Financial Planning Process 3
Short term and Long term Financial Planning 7
Financial Forecasting 10
Monitoring Activities 11
Risk Analysis 12
Summary 22

RESOURCE MANAGEMENT STRATEGIES 29
Financial Management 30
Human Resource Management 46
Information Management 53
Physical Assets Management 55
Materials Management 57
Summary 60

INCOME GENERATION 67
Maximising Income from Existing Sources 68
Using the Existing Customer Base to Raise Income 70
Identifying New Sources of Funds 71
Using Third Parties 73
Investing to Generate Income 74
Utilising Spare Capacity 75
Fundraising 76
Summary 79

COST BENEFIT ANALYSIS 85
Establishing Costs and Benefits 86
Measuring Intangible Costs and Benefits 89
Undertaking the Cost Benefit Analysis 92
Public versus Private Sector Service Delivery 96
Summary 98

ALTERNATIVE FINANCIAL STRATEGIES CONSIDERED 103
Devolvement, Business Units and Bank Accounts 104
Outsourcing, Tendering and Contracting 107
Providing More for Less 111
Community Choice 114
Maximising Income, Minimising Costs, and Building Reserves 117

SOLUTIONS TO EXERCISES 121

INDEX 137

Chapter 1

INTRODUCTION

In an environment where the demand for public services continues to grow, whilst often the financial resources cannot keep pace, managers need to become increasingly creative in the way financial resources are deployed by developing <u>realistic</u> financial strategies.

It may be considered that financial strategy should be left to the financial staff such as accountants, and finance managers, however, in organisations where operational managers often have devolved financial responsibility, they too need to be part of developing short and long term financial strategies.

This book considers how financial planning should be approached, such that appropriate financial strategies can be developed and implemented. Long range financial plans shape the future of the organisation and its ability to deliver the corporate, business and service plans. Financial planning should, therefore, be seen as an integral part of the overall planning processes. This text also looks at areas that are fundamental to supporting the financial planning process such as resource management, cost benefit analysis, and income generation. One option open to the public sector is to incorporate contracting out as part of a financial strategy to reduce costs. We consider the differences between public and private sector service provision, and the financial implications of both.

This book has been written as both a reference text and a development tool, which can be used by the reader as part of a self-development programme or to support recognised qualifications. At the end of each chapter are exercises and self-development activities, which can be undertaken by an individual or a team. The aim is to assist in interpreting the topics covered in each chapter as they are applied in practical and real life situations.

Strategic Financial Planning for Public Sector Services, provides stimulating ideas for managers to think strategically about how they plan and use the finances under their control, in order to shape future service delivery.

Chapter 2

FINANCIAL PLANNING

Financial planning is critical to the success of any organisation and should, therefore, be part of every planning process that has any financial implication. Within the public sector a great deal of emphasis is placed on financial control, but financial control can only be effective if there is a well thought out and robust financial plan against which to monitor performance. The more effort put into the financial planning process, the greater is the potential for effective financial control.

The Financial Planning Process

As with all plans, there needs to be clear aims, objectives, strategies, and implementation action plans which are constantly monitored and reviewed. Planning should always be an ongoing process, and this is no different for financial planning. Ongoing financial monitoring should highlight whether or not the financial plans are being achieved.

The financial planning process is illustrated in the following table.

The Financial Planning Process
- a continuous cycle -

STEP 1: Set objectives (may be for 1 or more years)

STEP 2: Develop strategies to achieve the objectives

STEP 3: Set out detailed action plans identifying targets, responsibility and timescales, along with detailed financial forecasts (budgets for income and expenditure, and cash flow forecasts if required)

STEP 4: Implement action plan

STEP 5: Monitor progress against planned targets and financial forecasts

STEP 6: Modify actions to reflect the current position, set new targets, produce revised financial forecasts, etc.

STEP 7: Review objectives to ensure they are still realistic and achievable

STEP 8: If necessary go back to step 1 and set revised or new objectives

---

Financial planning cannot be undertaken in isolation and should be performed in conjunction with the organisation's other planning activities. Most public sector organisations will develop a variety of plans setting out the key aims and objectives for at least the year ahead, if not for a longer period. The objectives identified in these plans will only be achieved if the financial resources are available to support them. The financial plans are critical in determining whether or not the objectives are realistic and achievable.

Depending upon how the organisation is structured, there may be a range of plans produced for a variety of purposes. Shown below is an illustration of the range of plans produced by public sector organisations and the type of financial plans that should be attached.

Type of Plan	Purpose	Financial Plan
Corporate Plan	Sets out the organisation's overall vision. It should give the organisation's general aims and key objectives that need to be achieved, and may be used as a framework for the development all other plans.	Should set out the planned income and expenditure for the whole organisation, clearly stating the sources of expected income and the key expenditure areas.
Best Value Plan	Requirements of its content are set down by the legislation. It has to be produced by all local authorities affected by the local government act 1999. Should set out how the authority intends to achieve Best Value from continuous improvement, how it is currently performing against target performance indicators, and how performance will improve.	The plan should have some financial information with respect to the authority's financial performance, and a budget based on the future plans for service improvement.
Departmental Business Plan	Within the context of the corporate plan, the department should specify departmental objectives, which should be SMART (Specific, Measurable, Achievable, Realistic and Time-related) in nature. It should identify how the department is organised and how the organisational structure will deliver the objectives. The action plans may be broadly based, but responsibility for achievement should be clearly defined along with timescales. This plan will provide the framework for all plans developed by the service units within the department.	The departmental budget should reconcile with figures produced in any of the other plans. How the budget is allocated between service areas, should be part of the departmental financial planning process. The budget allocation should allow service units to deliver the objectives identified in the plan. The financial plan should, therefore, provide details of the proposed income and expenditure for each operational or service unit, along with information on how the funding requirements for both revenue and capital expenditure will be achieved.

Type of Plan	Purpose	Financial Plan
Service (or Business) Plan	Most large organisations will organise their activities on the basis of service areas. These may be broken down into cost centres, business units, service units, etc. and it is now common for each service area to produce a service or business plan with respect to their activities. This plan should be more detailed than the plans previously mentioned such that they can be used as a working document. The content will include SMART objectives, strategies and action plans and should be used as part of the day-to-day management of the service. Service performance should be monitored on a regular basis against this type of plan.	The financial plan should be detailed with respect to month-by-month expected income and expenditure. It should ideally be profiled based on the planned service activities. The overall net expenditure budget, should agree with the service's budgeted expenditure set out in the departmental plan. The financial plan should be used as a regular monitoring tool for the service, and be part of the financial management and control process. There should be a clear link between service objectives, service output and the financial input. This can be achieved by adding a unit cost dimension to the financial plan such that productivity can also be monitored.
Operational Plans	In some organisations, there may be certain operations that cut across departments and/or service areas, and these operations also require plans. These tend to incorporate areas such as marketing, human resources, facilities management, communications, Best Value, contract management and so on. These operations may become business units in their own right, or may be co-ordinated functions spread across the whole organisation. The operational plans should take on a similar format to the business plans described above.	The financial plan for operations, may need co-operation and/or collaboration across a range of service areas or departments. The plan should be developed in the same manner described for the business or service plan. However, it is essential that the funding of operations is clearly identified, particularly where it is dependant on budgets arising from different sources.

In order to produce meaningful financial plans, there needs to be a mix of bottom-up and top-down communication as follows:

The corporate plan developed by senior managers, should be widely communicated such that all personnel understand the organisation's core objectives, the wider financial picture, and the available financial resources.

⇩

Service managers should then identify the level of financial resource they require, in order to deliver the objectives set out in their business plans.

⇩

When the service manager's financial plans are consolidated, the total financial requirement, at the service delivery end of the organisation, should fit within the organisation's overall financial resources.

⇩

Should the total requirement be greater than the available resources, this must be communicated downwards such that service managers can amend their business plans given the financial constraints.

Short term and Long term Financial Planning

Use of the phrases "short term" and "long term" planning vary considerably from organisation to organisation (the short term is often seen as 1 to 2 years, and the long term 3 to 5 years). In the public sector, however, the planning cycle tends to be short term, as long term planning often proves very difficult. Two important reasons for this difficulty are the funding regime (most funding is done on an annual cycle), and the political environment (involves regular Central and local government elections every few years). Given the types of services being delivered by the public sector, strategic financial planning should ideally span a longer period of time, incorporating both short and long term plans.

Shown below are some examples of long and short term financial objectives

Financial Objectives

Long Term Plan

1. To increase over the next ten years, the level of income directly generated to 20% of total income.

2. To ensure Council Tax rates are within the lowest 10% in the country (local authorities).

3. Over the next ten years, to increase the level of funds received from Europe by 15%.

4. To implement the ten year capital programme by self financing at least 30% of all capital expenditure.

5. To decrease overall debt levels by 8%, hence, reducing levels of capital charges and releasing more revenue for service expenditure.

Short Term Plan

1. All service areas to review their charging arrangements, with a view to generating an additional £200,000 this year, increasing by 10% year on year, thereafter.

2. For the following three years, ensure that council tax levels are increased at a rate less than the rate of inflation.

3. Establish a European office with the sole objective of identifying funding opportunities for the organisation, and raise at least £500,000 this year increasing this amount by 5% next year.

4. This year allocate £600,000 from reserves towards the capital programme.

5. Sell 1,000 properties this year and repay £5million of debt. New targets to be set annually depending on market trends.

Financial Strategies and Actions

It is likely that a range of financial strategies will need to be adopted in order to achieve the organisation's objectives. These strategies will often involve different parts of the organisation, not just the finance department. It is, therefore, important that financial strategies are developed and communicated to all departments, and where relevant, further disseminated to individual service areas. For example, the possible strategies for objective 1 above, are shown below.

Financial Strategies
Long Term Plan

Objective 1

Implement aggressive charging policies
e.g. ensure that charges are made wherever possible based on the ability to pay, and are set at levels to maximise income.

Tailor services for income generation
e.g. the way a service is presented will enable new or higher charges to be made.

For commercial services, adopt a profit maximisation pricing policy
e.g. ensure that for services which are not subsidised, the volume is maximised through competitive pricing policies.

Financial Strategies
Short Term Plan

Objective 1

Undertake market research on charging levels
e.g. undertake a customer survey with respect to services for which charges are currently made, and identify whether or not customers consider they are receiving value for money, and the scope to increase charges further.

Review all financial systems
e.g. ensure systems to raise and collect charges are sufficiently robust to maximise the level of recovery.

Increase charges above rate of inflation
e.g. where charging levels can be set by the organisation, add inflation plus a percentage this year.

In order to implement its strategies, the organisation must develop a range of specific actions. The most important aspects of an action plan is that it:

- relates to a specific objective
- is part of an overall strategy
- assigns responsibility to an individual or group of individuals
- sets timescales for completion
- sets targets, which can be monitored on a regular basis

Financial Forecasting

Having identified the objectives, strategies and actions of the financial plan, these need to be turned into detailed financial forecasts. Financial forecasts should be produced for both revenue and capital expenditure. They should include income and expenditure forecasts, which may take the form of a budget broken down between departments and services, and a cash flow forecast. Depending on whether or not cash flow responsibilities have been devolved within the organisation to departments or service areas, the cash flow forecast may only be produced centrally.

All forecasts should be based on a set of realistic assumptions taking into account the objectives and strategies set out in the financial plan. It is important that the financial plan is linked to service delivery and that all plans should be consistent with each other, such that coherant forecasts can be developed.

Detailed forecasts which accompany short term plans, should give a monthly breakdown of the figures and where possible, reflect the timing of income and expenditure using profiling techniques. The timing of receipts and payments should be reflected on the cash flow forecast. With respect to long term financial plans, the financial forecast are usually broken down on a quarterly basis for each forecast year.

Monitoring Activities

Financial planning is dependent upon a combination of what has happened in the past, the current situation, and future expectations. Therefore, monitoring activities form an essential part of the planning process, in so far as the results from monitoring are used to update the plan on an ongoing basis. Financial monitoring may be undertaken at a range of levels within the organisation, as follows:

Level	Financial monitoring responsibilities
Cost centre/business unit managers	Monitor their own budgets if operating in a devolved environment.
Service managers individually or as a team	Monitor the budgets of all the cost centres or business units in their service area, on an individual and consolidated basis.
Departmental managers individually or as a team	Monitor the departmental budget which should be an aggregate of all service area budgets, along with any support service budgets and central budgets that have to be recovered from departments.
Departmental finance officers	Depending on the organisation and the level of devolvement, individual departments, and sometimes even individual services or business units, may have finance officers who undertake financial monitoring. The monitoring activities undertaken at this level should be in support of the manager, as finance officers may not always be in a position to link service delivery to the financial performance being achieved.

Level	Financial monitoring responsibilities
Central finance officers	This financial monitoring is more strategic in nature, looking at the organisation's performance as a whole and identifying major exception areas that require explanation. The amount of detailed monitoring at the centre of the organisation, will vary depending on the level of devolved financial responsibility.

Monitoring should result in action which either enables objectives to be met or leads to changing priorities, and where necessary, changes to the objectives or strategies. It is also essential that lessons are learned from past performance such that future planning can take account of difficulties or changes that have been experienced.

Risk Analysis

Any financial plan by its nature, will have an element of risk, in so far as the outcome of the plan is uncertain. It is important for an organisation to assess the level of risk present in its planning, and make appropriate provision for each risk. Risk analysis looks at all the assumptions made when developing the financial plan which present an element of risk, and assesses the likely impact and gravity of those risks. This process is quite common in the private sector when predicting future income streams for both revenue and capital activities. Given that the public sector has limited resources, and in many cases less flexibility than the private sector with regard to its finances, analysing risk is very important. The typical type of risk affecting the financial plans of a public sector organisation are described as follows:

Income risk

For example:

- ❖ *Levels of grant expected - not always known in advance, and hence estimates have to be made*

- ❖ *Levels of fees and charges generated - estimates have to be made with respect to levels of demand*

- ❖ *Levels of interest earned on cash balances and investments - estimates have to be made with respect to average interest rates*

- ❖ *Levels of bad debts to be written off against income, estimates have to be made with respect to non payment of rents, council tax, fees and charges, and so on*

Service risk

For example:

- ❖ *Unexpected increases in demand for services - such as increase in birth rates, increase in life expectancy, major disasters e.g. train crash, etc.*

- ❖ *Larger than expected absenteeism level*

- ❖ *Changes in legislation directly affecting service delivery*

- ❖ *Poor performance and/or negligence leading to a detrimental impact on consumers - may lead to accidents, breaches in health and safety or other legislation, inadequate levels of care, financial loss, insurance claim, etc.*

Economic risk

For example:

- *Recession - leading to increased unemployment, homelessness, sickness, family breakdowns, reduced wealth and disposable income, etc.*

- *Restrictions on public borrowing - leading to difficulties in funding capital projects*

- *Large interest rate movements - high interest rates increasing the cost of capital, low interest rates affecting income from investments*

- *Inflation rate increases - will affect all estimates with regards to expenditure levels*

- *Taxation rate increases - this may have a large impact on expenditure levels if taxes increase on key supplies and services such as fuel, transport, and other consumables*

Political risk

For example:

- *Changes in political parties with different priorities that may require some public sector organisations to change their plans and strategies, including their financial plans*

- *Changing emphasis and funding for certain services based on a political agenda*

- *Legislation changes that directly affect public sector activities*

- *Government targets - may impact on an organisation's financial plans as it strives to meet the new targets*

> ## *Asset risk*
>
> For example:
>
> * *Under utilisation of property - resulting in a waste of resources*
> * *Dilapidations resulting in property or other types of assets no longer being fit for use, requiring investment in repairs or replacement*
> * *Premature obsolescence - leading to unplanned early asset replacement*
> * *Level of security - unsecured assets will be more susceptible to theft or criminal damage such as graffiti, smashed windows, etc.*

In order to assess the risk levels in each area, the organisation needs to make judgements as to the probability of different outcomes. The expected probabilities can be derived from:

* historical evidence
  (e.g. an assessment of what has happened over the previous five to ten years)
* official predictions by experts
  (e.g. interest rate growth, population growth rates)
* specific research
  (e.g. finding out customer preferences by way of questionnaires etc.)
* quantitative methods
  (e.g. calculating the range of possible outcomes and comparing them with the "normal" or "expected" outcome)

Strategic Financial Planning for Public Sector Services

- ❖ subjective methods
  (e.g. intelligent guess work based on one's knowledge or expertise)

Having identified the probability of different outcomes and the relative riskiness attached to the assumptions underpinning the financial plan, the risk analysis goes on to identify the impact of those risks on the robustness of the plan. Some elements may present virtually no risk, whilst others may be considerable. For example:

> The ambulance service for a large city, has embarked on a major overhaul of its planning processes and has identified in a long range corporate plan a number of key objectives to be achieved over the next ten years. These included the following:
>
> - At the end of the ten year period, to become one of the top 3 ambulance services in the country with respect to service quality and unit cost
> - To have completely replaced all vehicles with the most up to date models with on board state of the art equipment
> - To have launched a new air ambulance service with a private sector partner
> - To train all staff to paramedic standards, including support staff, and promote flexible working
> - To build reserves to a level of 10% of average net expenditure
>
> These objectives are ambitious given that the service currently has a very poor record on both quality and cost, a fleet of ageing vehicles, very few adequately trained staff and reserves barely equalling 1% of average net expenditure. The senior management team considered it important to develop a robust financial plan which would enable them to reach the targets. The financial plan objectives need to reflect the corporate objectives, and are set out as follows:
>
> - To reduce unit costs to the levels being achieved by comparative ambulance services, by reviewing all areas of expenditure and setting appropriate targets
> - To implement the most cost effective method of vehicle replacement

Strategic Financial Planning for Public Sector Services

- To raise private sector funding to invest in an air ambulance service
- To reduce expenditure on agency staff and recruitment
- To set budgets which achieve a net surplus year on year to contribute towards reserves

The key strategies to be used to achieve the financial plan objectives included:

- A review of all procurement methods in line with Best Value, to ensure the best possible prices are being achieved for goods and services being purchased from third parties

  This process is expected to result in a 15% revenue expenditure reduction on non employee costs

- Competitively tendering some of the support service activities such as the management of the staff canteen, facilities management, recruitment, and so on

  This process is expected to result in a net 10% saving on staff costs taking into account the cost of tendering and subsequent contract management

- Increasing productivity by introducing time sheets, performance related pay, incentives for low absenteeism and so on

  This process is expected to result in a 2% overall net saving on staff costs, mainly from the reduction in the use of temporary staff

- To approach private sector companies, who may have an interest in providing an air ambulance service, with the project plan to raise the required £2 million to purchase the air ambulance
- To devolve budgets and financial responsibility to cost centre managers with a target to generate savings, whilst increasing quality levels such as response times etc, as a result of the improved equipment and trained personnel that will be provided

These strategies should not only lower unit costs year on year, but also result in annual surpluses, assuming that funding increases by at least the annual rate of inflation, and that additional funding can be obtained to replace the vehicles

Strategic Financial Planning for Public Sector Services

The senior management team are all risk averse, and therefore wanted a risk analysis undertaken on the financial plan to ensure that the expected expenditure reductions and reserves growth, were really achievable. To undertake the risk analysis, they engaged an external firm of consultants to ensure objectivity

On examination of the financial strategies and the assumptions being made, the consultants identified and quantified the following areas of risk:

- Although there could be a 15% saving by changing procurement methods, the consultants considered there was a probability that such a saving could only be achieved for 80% of purchases, as 20% were already achieving lowest possible prices. Taking this probability into account, they consider that the overall saving to be 12% (80% of 15%)

- The consultants considered there was a very good market place for the tendering of support services, and achieving a 10% saving should be a prudent assumption. The main risk area will be the time taken to develop the specifications; appointing a provider; and starting the contracts. Any slippage will result in less overall savings over the period. Based on past experience, there is a 50% probability that there will be an average 6 month slippage, and hence this should be included in the financial forecasting

- The consultants suggested there was considerable risk attached to the assumption that productivity could be increased so significantly so as to save 2% on staff costs, even with the introduction of time sheets and performance pay. In fact, there could potentially be a net cost with respect to performance payments, not resulting in the reduced use of temporary staff. It was recommended that this approach be piloted in one area only to test whether the results did yield savings. The pilot would delay the scheme, but would provide reliable information with which to base future financial plans

- Although the air ambulance is a worthwhile project, the consultants saw two elements of risk. The first being whether or not the funds for purchasing the ambulance can be raised, and how long it would take to gain the support; it was recommended that a two year timescale be given for this in the financial plan. The second, was the support for the revenue expenditure to operate the air ambulance. This could result in increased expenditure if each year donors, sponsors or advertisers cannot be found. The consultants recommended a cost benefit analysis report on the project, and a fundraising strategy for the revenue costs, after which the riskiness of the project with respect to the financial plan could be re-appraised

- Devolvement tends to lead to a more efficient and effective use of funds, but not necessarily savings. However, the consultants did consider that devolvement should yield long term savings that would be difficult to quantify at this stage, but the financial plan could reflect savings targets that could then be monitored

The financial forecasts for ten years were developed taking into account the findings of the risk assessment, and the target level of reserves growth to 10% of net expenditure, revised downwards from the original objectives to 7.5%.

In order to protect the organisation from the consequences of risk, the financial plan should incorporate a number of safety nets. These may include:

Insurances	Policies can be taken out to cover many types of incident, however, there is an associated cost. An organisation must be decided whether the cost of insurance is greater than the potential risk occurring. It is advisable to obtain an independent assessment of the current level of insurance to ensure that it is sufficient to cover the most probable occurrences.
Alternative options	It is common for private sector companies to hedge against risk by developing alternative options, for example, should project A fail or be delayed, then project B would be activated to ensure any actual or potential losses are compensated for. This same approach can certainly be achieved in the public sector, especially with respect to capital projects. The financial plans may reflect expenditure on the ideal capital programme, but a range of alternative capital projects should also be developed in

case any project fails or cannot begin for whatever reason. On the revenue side, the same approach can be used. For example, organisations should develop alternative options to cover high levels of absenteeism, or ensuring there are back-up suppliers to cover the risk of non-performance of a service supplier.

Scenario planning — This requires the development of a number of plans reflecting different "what if" scenarios. This is a useful technique, because it ensures the organisation gives thorough consideration to the impact of different scenarios on their financial plans, and are ready to operate the correct plan given the relevant circumstances. For example, a local authority bidding for regeneration funds from Central Government, may create three different financial plans. Plan (A) assuming the bid is completely successful, Plan (B) assuming the bid is partly successful, and Plan (C) assuming the bid is unsuccessful. When the outcome of the bid is known, the correct financial plan can then be implemented immediately.

Contingency plans — The uncertain future results in a level of risk being attached to most financial plans. It is common to include a contingency within the plan to take account of such risks. The contingency level should be based on calculated risk, which can be estimated taking account of probabilities, and unforeseen risks which cannot be calculated because of their random nature. It is prudent to plan for savings such that an adequate contingency can be created. This may provide a better basis for the financial plan's success. For example, if a social services department develops financial plans which include forecast expenditure on children's homes, it is possible to calculate the risk of having to use more expensive homes given the nature of the client group. It may not, however, be possible to calculate the risk of a child needing more expensive secure accommodation due to the random nature of when this happens. Therefore, a contingency budget would enable both risks to be taken into account on the basis that it is unlikely that every potential negative outcome would occur at the same time.

Summary

- Financial planning should be undertaken in conjunction with other planning processes

- An organisation will develop a range of short and long term financial plans, to support other organisational plans such as the corporate and business plans.

- Financial plans should have objectives, strategies and actions in the same way as any other plan

- Detailed financial forecasts should be produced based on the financial plans. These forecasts should be supported by realistic assumptions which can be monitored on a regular basis

- All financial plans will have an element of risk attached, and this should be reflected in the financial forecasts. There are different types of risk that will have an impact on an organisations finances, including service, income and asset risk

- Organisations should take account of risk by considering insurances, contingencies, and alternative options for service delivery

Exercise 1

Developing Financial Strategies

Corrington Council have recently decided to adopt a new approach to financial planning. Historically they have always undertaken an annual budget setting process using a base budget, from which they deduct savings and add growth items in order to create the following year's budget. Outline budgets are developed for two further years using an assumed inflation rate and adjusted for any major planned changes.

The new approach combines business planning and financial planning such that the financial plans are in line with business plan objectives. Business plans and financial plans are supposed to be strategic in nature covering a three to five year period depending on the service. This will mean budgets will be set using a zero based approach rather than the traditional incremental approach.

The authority is divided into five strategic service areas: Education, Housing, Social Welfare, Community Services and Central Support Services. Each service area has a senior manager responsible for the business and financial plan, and they are expected to work as a team to ensure the plans are harmonised, economies of scale are achieved, and partnerships encouraged.

Joanne was recently appointed as the senior manager for Central Support Services, and has inherited the following annual performance:

Strategic Financial Planning for Public Sector Services

	Budget £'000	Actual £'000	Variance £'000	Current Position
Central Finance	760	840	-80	Overspending has occurred due to a large number of vacancies being filled with temporary staff; this is still the position. There is currently no intention to engage any further staff until a re-organisation has taken place
Internal Audit	440	490	-50	The volume of work has increased, and hence consultants have been engaged to assist. This was not in the budget and is not expected to re-occur
Legal	0	-10	10	As a self financing business unit, they have been able to make a small surplus most years
Human Resources	1,200	1,370	-170	Given the range of activities they have to perform, this service unit has historically been under funded. The only solution previously suggested, has been to outsource employment advertising, or something else
Democratic Services	390	450	-60	This budget is normally sufficient for operations. This year was an exception due to a number of member led initiatives requiring input from the department
Chief Executives	270	270	0	A purely staffing budget that is always on target
Public Relations	330	440	-110	The overspend is due to the demand for a much higher quality corporate image, including brochures etc. Also a Press Relations post was created, but not budgeted for
Contract Management	410	420	-10	This service is undertaken on behalf of departments, and expenditure should be fully recovered by way of re-charge to departments
Total	3,800	4,270	-470	

The above figures are for the year just ended. This year was a zero growth budget and spending patterns appear not to have changed. Joanne appears to be the budget holder, and service centre managers do not appear to own or take responsibility for their budgets or finance generally.

In the light of service requirements, Joanne has developed the following financial plan objectives that need to be achieved over the next three years:

- Expenditure on all budgets to be reduced by 10% at today's levels through efficiency savings and economies of scale
- Generate income equivalent to 5% of the current budget from third parties, by selling spare capacity to other public and voluntary sector organisations
- Use income generated over three years, to invest in upgraded computer systems and staff training
- Develop a contingency to target resources where they are most needed and to fund unforeseen peaks in workload
- Outsource any service unit that is unable to meet savings and income targets after three years, subject to cost benefit analysis

Questions

1. What financial strategies could Joanne adopt in order to achieve the objectives stated above?

2. What level of contingency should be set given the current figures?

3. What are the key risk areas that should be considered and taken into account with respect to Joanne's financial objectives?

Suggested solutions can be found on page 125.

Strategic Financial Planning for Public Sector Services

Exercise 2

Financial Planning in your organisation

Draw a chart or diagram that describes the financial planning process in your organisation, and highlight how it links into the key business plans produced by the organisation.

Reviewing the above diagram, list five ways in which you consider the process could be improved

1.

2.

3.

4.

5.

Chapter 3

RESOURCE MANAGEMENT STRATEGIES

A resource can be defined as *"a means to achieve an end"* (Concise Oxford Dictionary ninth edition).

The "end" is identified as the organisation's vision, aims and objectives, and the "means" to this end is usually one or a combination of the following resource areas:

- *finance*
- *human resources*
- *information*
- *physical assets*
- *materials*

The following paragraphs consider, from a financial perspective, management strategies for each of the above resource areas.

Financial Management

Strategic financial management should include:

- ❖ Achieving the long term financial objectives identified in the financial plan
- ❖ Monitoring key areas of expenditure by function (cost centre), and subjective (salaries, etc.)
- ❖ Financial decision making with respect to organisational over and under spending
- ❖ Long term investment strategies
- ❖ Ensuring adequate funding availability for capital expenditure programmes
- ❖ Effective cash management

Each of these issues are considered below

Achieving long term financial objectives

In the private sector, strategic financial management would tend to place emphasis on the over-riding objective to maximise profits, and the majority of financial management decisions are made on this basis. This may be tempered by the fact that in order to create large long term profits, there may be a need to undertake lower profitability or loss making activities in the short term. Strategic financial management would normally take the long term view, with financial management actions reflecting the strategic importance of profit maximisation over the long term.

It is clear, that even in the private sector, profit maximisation is not always the most influential objective. There are often other objectives, such as growth, which come into play and affect the financial management of the organisation. Some companies have an objective to be the largest and to dominate the market place in their field, even if this does not mean they are the most profitable. In the public sector there is a similar scenario. The over-riding objective of financial management, would usually be service maximisation. Service maximisation can be translated in different ways for different organisations. It may mean:

- the greatest quantity of service, given available funds
- the highest quality of service, given available funds
- the most cost effective services, taking account of efficiency and productivity
- or a combination of any of the above

When the organisation defines service maximisation, this simple maxim should provide a clear basis for financial decision making. However, as with the private sector, there may be other factors that make strategic financial management more difficult. These include:

Politics

There may be certain political objectives that affect the objectives relating to service delivery and result in financial resources being prioritised in a particular way. For example, due to public pressure, Central Government may set targets for health services to ensure that patients receive their operations within one month, even if this requires the use of private healthcare facilities. Unless additional funds are provided from Central Government for the new approach, the organisation may now have to manage financial resources in such a way as to ensure that the targets are met, even if it means diverting funds from other areas of service.

Personal Aspirations

Occasionally, individuals will seek to create short term gains at the potential sacrifice of the long term advantage. This affects the way in which finances are managed. For example, A Director of Housing may wish to invest in several new area housing offices which look impressive to the tenants, without due consideration to the on-going revenue costs of operating the new offices; clearly, these costs will have an impact on the finances of housing management services.

Maintaining the status quo and resisting change

This may be reflected in the objectives or the way objectives are interpreted by management and staff. The impact of this depends largely on organisational culture. It is particularly influential on financial management, if there is difficulty in making <u>radical</u> decisions which are necessary for the organisations successful long term financial management. For example, a social services department that is overspent every year, may need to make decisions to close down a number of nurseries and childrens homes in order to keep within the department's budget. However, because senior managers would rather not to make such difficult decisions, they resist making the necessary changes and the financial management of the service continues to be just as difficult as it was in previous years.

Cost minimisation

This objective would appear to be in line with value for money principles. The problem for financial management arises, when cost minimisation sometimes means input resources are substandard resulting in a poor service, with potentially expensive repercussions as a result. Minimising costs in some areas, may lead to additional costs elsewhere. For example, a fire service in their attempt to become more cost effective, changed all their suppliers of goods and services to the ones offering the lowest price. This resulted in poor quality parts for the fire engines, temporary staff with little commitment, and poor training. The results were considerable time delays in attending emergency calls because of a reduced number of operable vehicles and the need, on several occasions, to use neighbouring authority vehicles; additional expenditure which was not budgeted for, and hence financial management made difficult.

Contracting-out

Some organisations such as local authorities, have an objective to be an "enabler" rather than a provider of services. This objective results in a large number of contractors delivering services on the organisation's behalf. In theory it might be assumed that this makes financial management more straight forward as the cost of the contract is known, and the services to be delivered clearly specified. In practice, this may not be the case as contractors find many ways to charge for variations, or services are not delivered in accordance to the specifications. Added risks include the contractor's business failure that may lead to money and equipment being lost, as well as service disruption. For example, a hospital has a five year cleaning contract with a known private cleaning company. In year three of the contract, as a result of major changes to the hospital, including the addition of a new ward, the company has issued variations to the contract. Unfortunately, the original contract did not take in account rates for variations, and this has led to escalating cleaning costs resulting in large overspends on the cleaning budget.

Risk reduction

Many public sector organisations operate in high risk areas some of which could involve endangerment to life. Clearly, trying to reduce risk has an implication on finances. For example, in the provision of health care, preventative services may save money in the longer term, but the extent of the prevention may be difficult to quantify, and the case for spending on such services difficult to justify. Financial management can also become particularly difficult if an organisation experiences an incident as a result of poor services, or if they do not meet prescribed standards when inspected. The organisation would then need to ensure that the services were brought up to an acceptable level regardless of the cost. For example, an ambulance service, due to unusually high demand levels, found that the average response time of 20 minutes was well in excess of the performance targets. In addition, there were three fatalities in one month that were attributed to slow response times. The senior management team considered that performance targets must be met, and hence the risk of fatalities being attributed to slow respose times considerably reduced. This decision being part way through the financial year, will require all financial plans to be reviewed in order to identify the additional resources required to achieve this objective.

Some of these objectives are not necessarily in conflict with each other, but the impact on financial management can be considerable.

Monitoring Expenditure

The role of strategic financial management is to apply the standard monitoring techniques, such as variance analysis, projecting outturns, and so on, to the major budget areas. These can be divided into the main subjective areas as follows:

- *Employee Costs*
- *Accommodation*
- *Supplies and Services*

and the main functions

- *Departments*
- *Service areas*
- *Cost centres*

Effective monitoring of this nature, enables the organisation to identify areas of expenditure or income which are under performing, and to take the appropriate action. Unlike the monitoring that takes place at lower levels in the hierarchy, such as at cost centre level, which concentrates on individual items of expenditure, strategic monitoring will focus on:

Materiality:	Is the size of the over or underspend materially significant to the overall financial performance of the organisation
Bottom line:	Across the organisation, what impact is the net balance of over and underspending having on the bottom line surplus or deficit, and how does it relate to the target levels set in the financial plan
Fundamental changes:	Is the over or under spending position arising from a fundamental change which needs to be made to the financial plan's underlying assumptions, e.g. a major shift in demand, a change in legislation, etc.
Manageability:	Are departments able to manage the under and over spends being made, or do they require management from the centre
Strategic impact:	Will the current positions with respect to over and underspending, have a strategic impact on the ability of the organisation to achieve its short and long term objectives

Ideally, the organisation's existing monitoring processes will yield answers to the above questions. The information will enable those staff with strategic financial management responsibilities, the ability to make appropriate financial decisions. For example:

> The local police authority has invested in a number of key changes including a new integrated computer system, flexible working, new vehicles, and a newly refurbished police station. Most of the costs had been planned for, but unfortunately some areas of expenditure have exceeded the original budget. The central finance manager has

a strategic role and is part of the senior management team. The team depend on the finance manager for all aspects of financial planning, monitoring and control and tend to take her advice on most major financial decisions. Half way through the year, the financial manager, having undertaken the routine monitoring activities, has identified some major and significant overspends which have only just come to light. The reason being that invoices had not been promptly sent by some of the contractors. Having examined the variances and having projected the outturn, it appears that the refurbishment of the police station will be overspent by 20% by the time it is finished (£150,000), and the other key area of overspend is staff salaries (projected overspend £400,000). The overspend on salaries has arisen because of the extensive training programme that has been developed requiring a large amount of staff time at all levels. There have also been a number of new initiatives with respect to community policing and preventative work that has proved very labour intensive.

The financial manager has produced a report on the position, with a number of suggested actions that could be taken in order to manage the situation. These were as follows:

- Delay purchasing some of the new vehicles yet to be bought, and for the remainder of the year, continue to use some of the old fleet. Consider revising next year's financial plan to include the purchase of the outstanding vehicles. This strategy will have an impact on the vehicle repairs and maintenance budget, which was expected to be significantly lower than in previous years because of the new vehicle acquisition programme.

- Review the way in which the training programme is being delivered. Some of the training is essential, such as the equalities training, but other elements of the programme could be spread over a longer period of time, or postponed.

- Do not refurbish the administrative offices this year, hence reducing the refurbishment expenditure. Delay this until funds can be identified.

- Continue with the current position, and fund the differences out of the contingency budget usually held centrally for major accidents, peaks in demand for services, and other unforeseen events.

- Halt some, or all of the new initiatives which are not mandatory and still experimental.

All of the above potential actions have an element of risk attached to them, will have a strategic impact on the authority, and will result in some of the corporate plan objectives not being met. The senior management team will have to make decisions taking all these factors into account.

Financial decision making

Based on the organisation's financial monitoring activities, certain decisions will have to be taken in order to ensure finances are controlled in line with the financial plans. Public sector organisations have often found this aspect of financial management difficult, because financial decisions are regularly in conflict with worthy service decisions. This conflict means that difficult financial decisions are often put off until problems become critical, and at this time, the consequences are more serious than they would have been if earlier action had been taken.

Strategic financial decisions would tend not to focus on day to day, or operational issues, but more on ensuring the long term position remains viable and on target. The type of strategic financial decision may include:

- Whether or not to use reserves to fund short term overspends
- Which service areas should cease in order to achieve savings
- Where short term investments need to be made in order to generate long term savings
- The level and extent of savings required by each department in order to counter overspends
- Which are the most important priorities in the corporate/business plan, such that financial resources can be targetted appropriately

Strategic Financial Planning for Public Sector Services

- How should the financial plans be redesigned to take account of current circumstances, and what is the impact on the success or failure of the corporate/business plan

These decisions need to take into account the impact on:

- the level of risk
- the corporate/business plan objectives
- the financial plan objectives
- the planned financial strategies being adopted
- service delivery – quantity and quality
- customer perception
- the long term financial position of the organisation
- community and the environment

Continuing the previous example:

> Having considered the finance manager's report, and after much deliberation, the senior management team of the police authority decided on the following action plan:
>
> - To halt refurbishment to the administrative areas, as these parts would not be seen by the public, although there was acknowledgement on the negative impact it may have on staff morale
> - To slow down the delivery of the training programme by adding an additional year to the completion date, and prioritising both the elements of the training to be delivered and the range of staff that should attend first
> - To halt two out of the four community initiatives, and delay the start of one of the two preventative programmes
> - To try and finance any remaining overspends from cost centre savings, only using the contingency budget to balance the bottom line position if absolutely necessary

The finance manager was tasked to process these decisions and produce a revised financial plan and financial forecasts. The new plan and forecasts would then be used as a basis to monitor progress, ensuring that the decisions were having the desired effect.

Long term investment strategies

Strategic financial planning and management, must incorporate long term investment strategies. Public sector organisations are not in the business of taking risks with public money, even if they are in the fortunate position of being "cash rich". Unlike a private sector organisation, it is unlikely that a public sector organisation will have a financial objective of accumulating wealth, as they are generally in the business of service maximisation. However, it is usually in the organisation's best interest, to create prudent strategies that provide for the following types of objectives:

- Ensuring reserve levels are appropriate given the size and nature of the organisation
- Maintaining or improving quality standards
- Providing contingencies against risk
- Securing the value and replacement of assets
- Capital investment to save on revenue expenditure
- Capital investment to generate revenue income

There are a number of strategic issues to be considered in respect of long term investments, regardless of the objectives to be achieved. These include ensuring:

the cost of the investment does not outweigh the benefits whether they are tangible or intangible

(All investments have a cost, this may be the cost of capital itself; e.g. interest payments, or it may be the opportunity cost of investing monies elsewhere. Public sector organisations should be seeking to achieve a net benefit from any investment they undertake)

all the revenue implications of a capital investment have been fully considered

(An investment in property will result in ongoing revenue costs relating to the property such as rates, repairs and maintenance, insurances, and so on. These need to be incorporated into the financial plan post completion of the capital project)

the timescales associated with the investment are adhered to, e.g. ensuring projects do not overrun

(Some investments will be directly related to grant funding which if not utilised within a specific timeframe, will be withdrawn. Also, many investment projects will have a planned end date which will have implications for the organisation as a whole; e.g. an investment in a new computer system that has to be up and running by the beginning of the financial year, will have very severe consequences if it is late starting)

that the planned level of investment is not exceeded

(It is common for long term investment projects to go "over-budget". Many organisations accept over-runs as part of the process and develop "Contingencies" for such situations. However, public sector organisations are often not in a position to fund over spends without taking from other projects, and hence overspending can have a severe impact on the organisation's overall financial plans)

> **the investment programme has been planned to adequately meet current and future needs**
>
> (Long term investments often require a considerable planning time, and hence, it is quite common to find by the time the project is complete, it no longer meets current or future needs; e.g. properties constructed are too small for the numbers needing to use it, computer systems are not sufficiently powerful to meet the volume of user demands, road widening schemes still have insufficient lanes to handle the vast increase in road traffic, etc.)

> **where there is an investment choice, a proper appraisal has been undertaken to ensure funds are used in the most appropriate way**
>
> (Given that funds for investment projects are likely to be limited, there may be a need to choose from a range of worthwhile options, which project should be selected. It would be wise in such cases, for the organisation to use objective project appraisal techniques to choose between the projects, rather than a subjective approach; e.g. assessing the costs and benefits, calculating the net present values and rates of return, etc.)

It is clear that long term investment strategies will always have an element of risk attached, and this needs to be planned for as discussed in the earlier paragraphs on risk.

Long term investments need to be monitored and controlled in the same way as any other type of expenditure, and if there are problems, such as overspending, financial decisions need to be made to deal with these problems at the earliest opportunity.

Managers often view investment strategies as being part of a specialist remit, either at the centre or within a specialist department such as corporate finance or regeneration. As such, operational and service managers may feel divorced from this issue. However, in the light of Best Value and the fact that many public sector organisations, such as local authorities, are implementing devolved budgetary responsibility as a means of improving financial management and control, managers need to become more involved and aware of long term investment, and in particular, the impact it will have on their service area.

Financing Capital Expenditure

All capital expenditure, particularly long term investment projects of the type considered in the previous paragraph, require financing. The public sector has a variety of funding sources for capital projects, but does not have the same flexibility as in the private sector. The main sources of finance for such projects can be summarised as follows:

Borrowing
Many investment projects have to be financed by raising money from third parties in the form of borrowing. Obviously, considerations with respect to the cost of borrowing, and the terms of borrowing need to be taken into account. Central government also place restrictions on the levels of borrowing undertaken by the public sector, and may give guidelines as to the type of investments that can be made. For example, local authorities cannot invest in building social housing.

Grants
Central government, Europe, and other organisations provide grants for capital projects. These grants are usually given as a result of a bidding process, and often have restrictions attached as to the timescale and use of funds.

Reserves
Public sector organisations can accumulate reserves in the same way as any other organisation. It is quite common for organisations such as Housing Associations, to have large levels of reserves that can be utilised to fund capital expenditure. However, for many public sector organisations, the level of available reserves is often insufficient to consider funding any large or long term capital investment project.

Strategic Financial Planning for Public Sector Services

Leasing

This allows for the capital expenditure to be incurred by a third party, and the public sector organisation acquiring use of the investment on a lease rental or lease purchase basis. Leasing is commonly used to finance expenditure for items such as equipment, vehicles, technology, and so on.

Revenue expenditure

As the revenue expenditure for most public sector organisations is usually fully committed to direct service provision, this option would tend to be appropriate only in the case of small capital expenditure items or projects.

Private Finance Initiative (PFI)

This is a central government initiative designed to bring private finance into the public sector as a "modern way of investing", and "a key tool in helping to provide effective and good value public services". A PFI project involves the private sector making the investment in the project, with the public sector organisation entering a long term contract with respect to utilising the project. For example, a local authority requiring a nursing home service, could contract with a private sector company to build and run the nursing home. The authority would then contract to use the facilities for, say, a 15 year period. In some cases, central government may provide additional financial support for the project.

Public Private Partnerships (PPPs)

PFI projects are a form of PPP where the public and private sector work together in the provision of services. Again, central government are promoting this way of financing capital expenditure on the part of public sector organisations, as an innovative way forward bringing in not just private sector money but also their expertise.

Joint Ventures

Central government are encouraging public sector organisations to work with people in a number of ways. Joint ventures extend beyond the private sector to the voluntary sector and other public sector bodies. For example, if the health authority and the local authority could both benefit from building a local health and family centre, it is strategically sound to undertake the project as a joint venture, sharing the costs and maximising the use of the centre when it is complete.

Strategic Financial Planning for Public Sector Services

In funding capital capital projects, public sector managers should be aiming to maximise the use of the financial resources under their control, and therefore need to be creative in the way future projects are financed.

Effective Cash Management

Cash is essential to the efficient and effective running of all organisations and is crucial to pay for staff, supplies and services, contractors, and so on. This often requires public sector organisations to have overdraft and other short term loan facilities. These facilities need to be used if cash outflows are exceeding cash inflows at any particular point in time. In order to ensure that cash is being managed effectively, public sector organisations should have the following systems in place:

Treasury management	This usually refers to the short and long term management of cash and cash like resources, and is a critical tool in the strategic financial management armoury. Although public sector organisations should not make risky investments, treasury managers can seek to maximise their income from cash resources by skilfully monitoring cash balances and keeping close control over cash flows. In order to maximise income from treasury management there needs to be: • Regularly produced and updated cash flow forecasts such that the organisation can have a good approximate idea of what levels of cash are needed and when. • Regular monitoring of interest rates on all types of short to medium term investments, such as overnight deposits, longer term deposit accounts, treasury bills, etc. • Regular monitoring of overdrawn balances and short term loan positions. These should be kept to a minimum as they would tend to cost more than that earned on cash investments

Treasury management (continued)	• Use of different bank accounts for different activities, with a view to minimising bank charges; for example, some capital projects may warrant separate bank accounts with different terms • Use of staff skilled in the area of treasury management
Debt collection and recovery	The rate at which debts are collected and recovered, has a direct impact on treasury management discussed above. The more effective the debt collection and recovery systems, the greater the cash inflows and the less need for short term borrowing to cover cash deficient periods. Local authorities, in particular, often have high levels of debt in the form of rent and council tax arrears. In order to maximise the cash receipts from outstanding debtors, there needs to be: • A clear recovery process in force that is understood by staff and customers, e.g. everyone is educated about each stage of the recovery process in advance of any transaction • A willingness to implement recovery stages as soon as possible once a debt becomes over due, so as to maximise the chance of recovery, e.g. charging interest, chaser letters, bailiffs, etc. • Where appropriate, incentives to encourage people to pay on time or even in advance e.g. discounts, free prize draw, etc. • In order to collect cash more quickly, incentives to encourage people to pay by direct debit or standing order • Accurate and timely charging mechanisms, e.g. customers will have a good excuse not to pay if errors are made
Grant claims	• Any income maximisation strategy would include maximising the amount of grant income. Most grants require claim forms to be completed, some of which may be complex in nature and require the input of finance staff. Obviously, the sooner a grant is claimed and received, the better this is for cash flow. Some public sector bodies have most of their income in the form of grants, and hence cash flow is very dependant on efficiency in this area. Inefficiency will cost money in the form of interest on short term borrowing. In order to ensure the efficient cash inflow from grants, one should:

Strategic Financial Planning for Public Sector Services

Grant claims (continued)	• Where possible, negotiate grant payments in advance as opposed to in arrear • Develop a timetable setting out when grant claims have to be submitted, and the lead time required to prepare the relevant information and documentation • Establish data collection systems that make grant claim submissions easy to prepare • Ensure all staff involved in preparing or providing information for grant claims, are aware of the timetable and have been given individual targets to complete their aspect of the claim • Where possible, establish arrangements to receive grants by automatic transfer to save the time of issuing, sending and banking cheques
Tax management	Public sector organisations have to pay tax on goods and services, and can in some instances reclaim the tax paid. Reclaiming tax has a cash flow implication, and again the efficiency with which this is undertaken can have a positive impact on cash management, and the ability of the organisation to use this as a means of generating income as opposed to expenditure. To ensure that tax management is effective, there needs to be: • A clear understanding of what taxes can be reclaimed • Efficient processing of information and timely submission of tax claim forms • An understanding by all staff of the importance of record keeping, and the fact that even small purchases from petty cash may include tax which can be reclaimed if a tax receipt is retained

Human Resource Management

This is usually the largest area of expenditure in any public organisation, as is the case with any service based business. With respect to strategic human resource management, the key areas which have a strategic financial consequence are:

❖ Use of agency staff (temporary staff engaged from an employment agency)

- Use of vacant posts
- Use of training and development
- Use of productivity monitoring and unit costing

Agency Staff

There are occasions when agency staff have to be engaged, such as to maintain staff to client ratios in certain service areas. In most sectors, agency staff are more expensive than a permanent staff member as the employment agency providing the staff, charges a commission on top of the basic rate of pay. Due to the costs and other factors involved, organisations often attempt to keep the use of these staff to a minimum. This can be achieved by:

- Introducing flexible working practices, whereby absenteeism can be covered by other staff who are trained in the appropriate area of work, and who are able and prepared to work overtime hours
- Innovative use of rotas and shift working
- Planning annual leave such that cover can be provided internally, e.g. restricting the amount of annual leave that can be taken during busy times of year
- Developing an internal bank of permanent staff whose role is to fill in gaps as they arise, (a model used by private sector firms who have permanent staff, whose role is to take temporary positions within the organisation as and when required)
- Developing an external bank of temporary staff, with terms and conditions more favourable to the organisation than using staff from private sector agencies. Some public sector organisations have developed their own in-house agency

Strategic Financial Planning for Public Sector Services

In certain circumstances, agency staff can be used strategically as a way of reducing costs, providing more flexibility in the way services are provided, and increasing efficiency levels when used to cover peaks in workloads. The benefits arise because:

- There is no need to pay agency staff for any absenteeism resulting from sickness, holidays and so on

- There is no commitment to provide staff benefits such as pensions, car allowances, health insurance etc.

- The staff member will only be engaged for as long as is required, so there is no ongoing commitment to meeting regular salary payments

- Poor quality agency staff can be dismissed immediately and replaced by the agency

- In some areas, agency staff rates are less than those of permanent staff rates, (e.g. areas such as cleaning and domestic services) particularly when staff benefits etc are taken into account

- Productivity can be specifically monitored as time sheets have to be produced and authorised

Consider the following example:

> The prison service let a contract to manage three prisons, to the in-house team of one of the prisons who had formed themselves as a not for profit organisation called Prisons Unlimited Group, (PUG). This tender was won against competition from private sector companies, and had been let for the duration of five years with an option to extend for a further five years subject to certain targets and performance indicators being met.
>
> Two of the prisons had historical staffing problems. Overspending on employee costs occurred every year and was sometimes as high as 20% of the staffing budget. The main cause being the use of agency staff that were never budgeted for, but were always used as staff to prisoner numbers have to be maintained.

When preparing their bid, PUG saw this as a key area for savings and their strategy was to drastically reduce the spending on agency staff by using the fact that with three prisons under management, they could gain economies of scale. They intended to:

- Set up a bank of well trained multi-skilled permanent staff, who would be prepared to work flexibly between the three sites
- To reduce the number of permanent staff based at each site by 15%, to account for fluctuating occupancy rates. Temporary staff on short term contracts would be engaged to supplement staff numbers when full occupancy is reached
- Give staff enhanced rates for overtime pay which will be lower than agency rates
- Revise rotas to make more effective use of staff
- Encourage job sharing and part-time working
- Introduce flexible working patterns whereby staff learn different job roles within their grades, and familiarise themselves with each of the three sites

Even with these changes, there was recognition of the need to use agency staff to a very limited degree to cover for any unplanned events, hence a small budget was established for very limited occasions. The selected agencies were all required to produce competitive prices.

This approach enabled PUG to meet all the required staffing standards as laid down in the specification, with an overall employee cost which was 5% lower than the previous year's budget.

Vacant Posts

It is quite common for public sector organisations to use vacancies as a way of managing staffing budgets. Obviously, there is a saving if a permanent member of staff is not replaced immediately, however, as a strategy to reduce expenditure, it is clearly flawed if that post has to be covered by using temporary staff or overtime, which are usually more expensive options. Also, if the organisation is an efficient service provider, a vacancy should result in a reduction in service output, which will affect performance indicators and quality standards. Efficient recruitment to vacant posts, as soon as they occur, should ultimately save money and increase efficiency.

Vacant posts can be used as a management tool and part of a financial management strategy, in the following circumstances:

- Where the post would be redundant and does not need to be replaced, a permanent saving may be achieved
- Where the service is being subject to a review involving changes to the structure and number of staff, resulting in the vacancy not being filled, or staff being changed to a lower grade and salary
- Where average demand for the service has fallen, and the vacant post can be filled on a part time or temporary basis to meet peaks in demand when they arise
- Where the vacant post can be filled by more junior but able personnel, a marginal saving can be made

Training and Development

Investing in training is an important element of the financial strategy, as there are generally long term financial benefits to having well trained staff. However, along with other "invest to save" strategies, expenditure today will not necessarily yield beneficial results until a much later date, therefore, investment in training is sometimes a difficult choice for the public sector which has traditionally focused on short term financial planning.

Training and staff development can vary from expensive professional qualification training, which may take several years to complete, to short skills development workshops which may be half a day in duration, and delivered in-house. The key purpose of training and development, must be to create a workforce that is best able to deliver the organisational objectives. Arising from this objective, the types of economy which are achieved by investing in training and development include:

- Increased accuracy, hence reduced waste
- Increased levels of productivity, and therefore a need for less staff to fulfil the same amount of work
- Increased efficiency and effectiveness leading to higher quality standards and less service risk
- Can develop trainee posts at lower cost, with the incentive of promotion when training completed
- Increase staff retention, and hence saving in recruitment cost and induction training
- Lower levels of absence, reducing expenditure on temporary cover and overtime payments

To maximise the benefit from the training investment, the organisation should ideally have a strategy of succession planning and enabling staff to be promoted into key positions over time. This would lead to "home grown talent" with high skill levels, historical knowledge of the organisation, its goals, its culture, and working practices. In the public sector, the ability to operate such strategies can be limited depending on the employment practices which are in place.

Productivity and Unit Costs

Human resource management should include strategies around staff productivity and unit costs, both of which have a direct impact on the effectiveness of the financial strategies. Monitoring productivity has always been a difficult subject, as many staff tend to dislike, and in some instances distrust, the introduction of timesheets or target output quotas etc.

Unfortunately, productivity can only be properly monitored with some kind of record keeping with respect to how staff are using their time. These time records can then be used to calculate unit costs which give a true gauge of whether or not a best value service is being delivered, and if resources are being deployed to best effect. When effectively undertaken, the introduction of time recording tends to:

- ❖ Increase time spent on productive activities
- ❖ Make staff consider more carefully how they are using each hour of their time, and become accountable for their actions
- ❖ May result in changes to job descriptions, working practices and procedures
- ❖ Helps reduce the time spent on wasteful activities, e.g. people begin to question the amount of time spent in meetings and the necessity of those meetings as a form of communication
- ❖ Identifies the real cost of certain services, e.g. often organisations are surprised to learn that services which are not the highest priority or most strategic are the most costly.

The use of time recording can be further enhanced with the introduction of an appraisal system, which focuses on performance monitoring and target setting.

Time recording does have a negative side, insofar as it takes time to complete time records, collate time information, and to analyse the information being collected. In addition, some staff also feel it inhibits their ability to freely perform their duties, it is an unnecessary intrusion into their work routine, and are suspicious as to how the information will be used.

Information Management

Information is a critical resource for all organisations, especially those delivering public services. It provides:

- Data needed on a daily basis to deliver the service, and to function as an organisation
- An historic record of past service delivery and operations
- Data that can be used for future planning

Given the reliance which most organisations have on information, it becomes of strategic importance to create and utilise systems that can effectively manage information. All information systems, automated or manual, should have the following features:

- Accurate and complete data entry to the system
- Processing facilities that sort the information in an appropriate manner for the user
- Simple retrieval mechanisms such that information is readily accessible
- Flexible reporting procedures such that relevant and timely reports can be produced on demand

Typically, organisations will invest in ensuring certain key systems are in place, however, many public sector organisations sometimes lack adequate systems, or do not fully utilise their existing systems. The types of information system present in the public sector include:

Financial accounting systems
(to record financial transactions and produce financial accounting information for internal and external purposes)

Financial management systems
(to provide financial planning, forecasting, budgets and budget monitoring information for internal purposes)

Management information systems
(to provide service data such as productivity, output, time recording, employment data, customer databases, workflow, etc.)

Specialist operational systems
(to support particular service activities such as pensions, social services care management, housing management, etc.)

Most organisations will have computerised information systems, some of which will still require support from manual systems, (although ideally, there should be no need for duplication). Information from these systems will be required for:

- Benchmarking
- Best value reviews
- Unit costing
- Business and service planning
- Marketing

Harnessing information is a valuable resource and the financial implications are considerable. Not having the available information can lead to poor decision making and costly mistakes, whereas decisions made on sound information may lead to savings. The development of the Internet and Intranet, now enables the quick and easy access and transfer of information from internal and external sources. The public sector needs to be at the forefront of these developments as they will revolutionise the way in which many public services are delivered in the future. This is already being demonstrated in areas such as:

Transportation – ticket purchases, timetables, etc.

On line selection and payment for goods and services including council tax and parking fines

Information booths – instead of one-stop shops to provide local area information, and so on..

These developments can only be achieved by investment in practical information systems.

Physical Assets Management

The financial definition of physical assets is "those items that have an ongoing value to the organisation". These are included in the fixed asset categories of the financial accounts, and typically include:

- Land and Buildings (all property assets including major improvements to property)
- Furniture, Fixtures and Fittings
- Equipment
- Vehicles
- Plant and machinery

Expenditure on these areas is referred to as capital expenditure.

Most public sector organisations spend a large amount of money on capital expenditure in the form of an annual capital programme, and some have a large amount of their financial resources tied up in the form of these assets, particularly property. The amounts involved can be seen on the financial accounts of any public sector organisation. The way in which physical assets are purchased and then managed, may have a considerable impact on an organisation's financial strategy.

Strategic considerations with respect to physical assets include:

Buying versus renting	Depending on the circumstances, either strategy may be appropriate. The option to buy will only be possible if financial resources are available by way of loan, sale of other long term assets, PFI/PPP, grants, or internal funds such as reserves. Renting has implications on annual revenue expenditure for the duration of the rental agreement. The manager needs to consider the benefits of each in relation to the asset requirements. For example, the benefits of buying are ownership, control, appreciation in value (property), flexible usage, etc., whereas the dis-benefits include repairs and maintenance, insurance, depreciation (vehicles), obsolescence, ongoing commitment to running costs regardless of usage.
Leasing	This is another way of financing assets and is usually used with respect to vehicles, plant, machinery, and equipment. Leasing enables organisations to acquire assets where it would not wish to buy outright, or there are insufficient funds to do so. There is of course a cost to leasing which may be more expensive that loan financing, depending on the applicable interest rates at the time.

Use of assets	If a public organisation owns buildings or other assets that are not being fully utilised, there is an obvious waste of resources. For example, there may be many reasons why buildings may become under utilised, such as reduced demand, change in service requirements, disrepair, etc. Where, the role of the organisation is clearly not that of landlord, and when landlord activities become greater than the service, action should be taken to consider the continued viability of owning such assets.
Sale of assets	Public sector bodies have opportunities to realise capital gain through the sale of property. Often properties have been owned for many years and have appreciated considerably in value. In the same way that the strategic down-sizing of the number of bank branches have resulted in the sale of many bank premises, local authorities, for example, are selling town halls and other civic buildings. The monies received from the sale, often referred to as a capital receipt, can be used to repay loans, invest in new property, fund repairs to other properties, and so on. Local authorities have restrictions on how capital receipts can be used and these are laid down by central government. Other assets usually depreciate in value, and therefore an organisation should maximise the use of that asset up to and beyond its useful life, as defined in the accounts.
Asset management	Facilities management, fleet management, and so on are specific disciplines in their own right. Many public sector organisations have in-house service departments that undertake this work, however, this has been a key area for contracting out to the private sector. In fact, public sector organisations should now be questioning their roles with respect to asset management. For example, with respect to local authorities it is now common for tenant management boards to manage their own estates. In this way the authority is divesting itself of the management and other responsibilities which come with the ownership of such properties.

Materials Management

For those private sector companies which are heavily reliant upon materials to produce goods and services, this is a major area of resource management. This includes most manufacturing sectors, building and construction, and retail.

In such industries, disciplines such as stock control, order quantities, discounts, and vertical integration with suppliers are all key issues. The public sector being a service industry, does not rely so heavily on materials for service delivery, however, materials is an important resource in some areas and many public sector organisations buy in other resources such as temporary staff. The management of materials and similar inputs to service delivery are important to the overall effective use of financial resources.

The main areas that need to be considered with respect to materials management are as follows:

Purchasing arrangements
Public sector organisations have strong purchasing powers and can, therefore, insist on discounts for large volumes etc. Other areas of negotiation should include price fixing for a specific period, favourable payment terms to assist with cash flows, (e.g. at least 30 day credit terms), lower prices for block contracts. If preferred suppliers lists are used, they need to be updated at least annually to ensure the best suppliers and prices are those on the list.

Stock holding levels
Ideally all stock should be kept to a minimum, as there is a cost to holding stock, which includes storage costs. With good work flow systems, a "just in time" approach could be used. However, there should always be a minimum quantity level set for re-ordering such that stock outs are avoided. For example, in a doctor's surgery, being out of stock of disposable gloves, could have severe consequences on the GP's ability to perform even the most basic treatment.

Quality control
This is critical to the effective use of resources. If the materials used in the production of goods and services are sub standard,

it invariably leads to a substandard product or service. Even though it may not be the organisation's fault, it has a duty of care to ensure that the goods and services given to the public meet certain standards. For example, if a leisure centre utilised poor quality safety equipment and an accident occurred as a result of such equipment, this incdient could have a serious impact on the organisation, resulting in higher insurance premiums etc.

Summary

- Strategic financial management should include the achievement of financial objectives

- The most important objective for most public sector organisations is service maximisation. This, however, needs to be defined and it can then be used as a basis for financial management decision making

- Financial monitoring, at the strategic level, should take account of materiality and the impact on the bottom line

- Effective cash management is essential to all organisations and incorporates treasury management, debt collection, grant claims and tax management

- The largest area of expenditure for the public sector is employees, and effective human resource management can have a significant impact on the organisation's financial position

- Other resources which have a financial impact and require careful management include information, assets, and raw materials

Strategic Financial Planning for Public Sector Services

Exercises 3

Financial Decisions

You are the new Director of Finance taking up a position that had been vacant for the last 3 months. It is currently mid way through the financial year, and a number of resource issues have come to light where your input into the decision making is critical. The organisation's overriding objectives are to ensure budgets are not breached and service levels are maintained.

You have been presented with the following list of problems, along with a number of options in each case, and you are expected to give guidance as to the best decisions to take in the interest of the organisation's long term financial position.

a)

Problem	Options
The capital programme is in trouble. One project with a value of £2.5m is delayed by 6 months, and 3 projects are due to exceed budget by 10% totalling £1m	(a) Begin a substitute project and use the £2.5m within the timescale. Seek to raise the £1m overspend from sale of assets (b) Use £1m to fund the overspends on the 3 projects, and identify another project to utilise £1.5m (c) Review the overspending budgets with a view to bringing expenditure back on track. If possible invest the £2.5m until the project can be started
Decision	

Suggested solutions can be found on page 127.

61

Strategic Financial Planning for Public Sector Services

b)

Problem	Options
The employees budget appears to be overspent by 10% due to the heavy dependence on temporary staff provided by agencies	(a) Renegotiate contract arrangements with agencies and force down rates, otherwise do not use the agency
	(b) Recruit and fill vacancies, allow services to decline in the short term to generate savings
	(c) Establish an in-house bank of staff to cover absences and cease use of agency staff
Decision	

c)

Problem	Options
Two properties have been put up for sale by auction and failed to meet their reserve prices (£300,000 each). They are both in a poor condition and require £250,000 investment in repairs. Doing nothing will result in the values declining and the cost of repair increasing	(a) Re-auction with a lower reserve price
	(b) Fund repairs by cutting an alternative capital project, undertake the repairs, and re-auction at a higher price
	(c) Seek partnership funding to undertake the repairs, and bring buildings temporarily back into use until property prices increase
Decision	

d)

Problem	Options
A major service area, relating to a statutory responsibility of the organisation is to date overspent by £2million, on a budget of £12million for the year. Overspending in this area has been a major cause of the organisation's deficits for the last 3 years. The position has to be rectified	(a) Fund overspend from reserves and from next year ensure budgets are set from a zero base, and truly reflect the necessary expenditure
	(b) Calculate the expected outturn and the total expected overspend for the year. Cut expenditure on other non statutory services to fund overspend. Revise content of service to minimum level for future years so as to reduce expenditure
	(c) Take personal responsibility for this budget and gain a real understanding of why budget overspends are occurring. Accept the reality of another deficit year, but ensure strong control introduced for the future
Decision	

e)

Problem	Options
Outstanding debtors are currently £35million, which is £5million more than target. This has lead to an overdraft of £3million, which is the limit currently available to the organisation. The position appears to be deteriorating rather than improving	(a) Implement a stronger credit control and collection policy, outsourcing if necessary
	(b) Negotiate a new overdraft limit with existing bankers or change banks
	(c) Introduce incentives for advance payments, such as discounts, charge reductions, and so on
Decision	

Strategic Financial Planning for Public Sector Services

f)

Problem	Options
A piece of land for which planning has been granted for the development of housing is to be sold, however, the highest bidder is likely to be a private developer for luxury apartments and not the social housing sector, for which there is a great need in the area. A substantial profit on sale could be realised (up to £10million) depending on the selected purchaser	(a) Take the highest bidder in order to maximise profit and build reserves/fund overspends (b) Initiate a partnership between the private and social housing sector to allow for some social housing as part of the development, whilst maintaining a high bid price (c) Maximise bid price from the social housing sector even though profits may be lower, a significant contribution will still be obtained
Decision	

g)

Problem	Options
The Director of Human Resources has identified a desperate need to train managers and consider it an essential part of the strategy to increase efficiency, service quality and performance. Central funding is being requested this year to pay consultants to develop the programme. The Xfile consultants require £250,000 to begin the project and were the only bidders	(a) Agree to the expenditure and fund it by using reserves or making expenditure savings in service areas (b) Insist on retendering with a repackaged specification to encourage more bidders, with a view to reducing the cost (c) Delay the whole programme to next year when provision for it can be made in next year's financial plan
Decision	

Strategic Financial Planning for Public Sector Services

Exercise 4

Resource Management in Practice

Drawing on your own experience, and using the following table, set out the strengths and weaknesses for each of the resource areas and using this assessment, identify the strategies that should be implemented.

Resource	Strengths	Weaknesses	Strategies
Finance	e.g. Reserves of £25m	Continuous overspending	Introduce zero based budgeting and accurate profiling
Cash	e.g. Positive liquidity ratio	Overdraft position increasing	Introduce tougher credit control and debt collection procedures
Human Resources	e.g. Good management development programme	High levels of agency staff	Review pay and benefits package of vacant posts

Strategic Financial Planning for Public Sector Services

Resource	Strengths	Weaknesses	Strategies
Information	e.g. High level of data collection	Data not easily retrievable	Introduce an integrated data management system
Assets	e.g. High value property in good condition	Underutilisation	Consolidate use of strategic sites and rationalise number of properties
Materials	e.g. Low level stock holdings	Inefficient purchasing	Incentivise purchasing department to achieve Best Value

Chapter 4

INCOME GENERATION

Many public sector organisations adopt financial strategies that concentrate on how to achieve savings through the existing expenditure. Although these strategies are very important, particularly with respect to striving towards the 3E's (efficiency, effectiveness and economy), they are not the only possibilities. There are a number of income generation strategies that should also be considered, such as:

- Maximising income from existing sources
- Using the existing customer base to raise income
- Identifying new sources of funds
- Using third parties
- Investing to generate income
- Utilising spare capacity
- Fundraising

We consider each of the above income generating strategies in the following paragraphs.

Maximising Income from Existing Sources

This strategy is just good house-keeping and an important area to focus on for some organisations that are actually losing income due to inefficiencies, such as submitting grant claim forms late or incorrectly. Some public sector organisations will have a range of income sources, and although some may be far more important in terms of their size, they should all be subject to the same strategy of maximisation. The typical sources of income include:

Income sources	Maximisation strategy
Grants	Grants come from a range of sources such as central government, government quango's, major charities, Europe, and international organisations. In all cases, there is a need to complete application forms or give returns with respect to how grant funds have been used. Grant funding usually has conditions attached which must be fulfilled, and monies can be lost if these conditions are not adhered to. In order to maximise income from grants, the organisation should: • Identify all potential areas where grant funding may be applicable • Apply for all grants that need applications well within the due dates • Ensure that all terms and conditions of grant are adhered to • Ensure that all returns with respect to how grants have been utilised are accurately completed by the due date • Ensure that all financial accounts in respect to grants are completed by the due dates, and audited (if required) • Pro-actively form good relationships with grant givers, and ensure that there is a positive awareness of the need for funding • Lobby appropriate government departments and organisations responsible for the allocation of grants

Strategic Financial Planning for Public Sector Services

Income sources	Maximisation strategy
Fees & Charges	For some public sector organisations, this may be the major source of income. Fees and charges are raised for all kinds of services including, nursery places, residential homes, leisure centres, planning applications, homecare, fines, and so on. To maximise the income generated from fees and charges, the organisation should: • Constantly review pricing levels such that the rates reflect the market demand and supply, are consistent with the rates of competitors or similar service providers, and provide value for money (Some charges may be controlled by government or regulators, and the organisation may have to take into account affordability and ability to pay) • Ensure the services delivered meet the required standards such that fees are justified • Ensure the productivity of chargeable activities is as high as possible, such that the volume of fees and charges are maximised • In order to maximise payments, ensure a proper billing and collection system exists • Consider a pro-active marketing strategy to promote fee generating activities, ensuring that the cost of marketing is more than covered by the expected increase in the level of fees • Where appropriate, use techniques to encourage volume, e.g. bulk discounts, introduction incentives (e.g. get a friend to join the leisure centre and you receive a bottle of wine), special offers and promotions
Rents	Rental income will arise in many public sector organisations, from a college letting a room to local drama groups, to a local authority housing department collecting rent from thousands of tenants. In order to maximise income from this area, the organisation should: • Identify properties available for letting and ensure that they are in a lettable condition, and minimise the number of void properties by ensuring all vacant properties are brought into letting as quickly as possible

Income sources	Maximisation strategy
Rents (continued)	• Set rents at levels which reflect the market place, and are comparable to other similar rentals (in the case of social housing, affordability may be a key parameter) • Ensure there is an efficient and effective billing and collection service in place • Provide incentives for prompt payment of rents, and severe penalties for late and non payment
Interest	As mentioned in the resource management chapter, effective treasury management is key to maximising the amount of income generated in this area
Sector specific revenue	Some public sector organisations have certain specific revenue sources, for example, local authorities can raise income from local taxes, and police authorities are precepted from local authorities. An income maximisation strategy for a local authority, would be to charge as high a local tax as possible, within central government constraints. This financial strategy is often in conflict with a political strategy whereby the Council Members, who are the ultimate decision makers would consider it an unpopular strategy which may affect their standing with voters. Other areas of the public sector will also have specific sector related revenue income, which they need to assess with respect to a maximisation strategy

Using the Existing Customer Base to Raise Income

Even though public services are often provided to meet needs and are not necessarily charged for on an itemised basis, the service users still form a customer base. This customer base can be a source of income in the following ways:

⇨ **They can be sold other goods and services**
    (e.g. this has been done successfully by hospitals which now have semi-shopping malls attached to them; whether the organisation sells franchises to recognised retailers or retails directly, income is generated)

- **They can be used for fundraising**
  (e.g. it is common to have charitable boxes, etc at reception points where people are waiting for services)

- **They can be recruited as volunteers to assist with elements of service delivery**
  (e.g. this may result in a cost saving and quality enhancement to the service)

- **They can be charged for enhanced and ancillary services**
  (e.g. some users of meals on wheels services would be prepared to pay more for a gourmet menu, or be prepared to pay for a more specialist shopping service. Schools can charge for after school programmes and summer projects)

- **They can be used as advocates to promote services and increase usage**
  (e.g. Leisure centre members may receive one month's free membership if they can recruit another person)

- **They can be incentivised to continue to use, or extend their use of income generating services**
  (e.g. private and voluntary sector groups paying rent for the use of community centres, schools, etc., may be offered a discount if they book the venue for a year at a time)

- **They can be forced to join certain fee paying schemes in order to continue receiving the service**
  (e.g. local authorities may insist on businesses using specific refuse sacks if their rubbish is to be collected, and the refuse sacks have to be purchased for an additional fee.)

Identifying New Sources of Funds

This is a more difficult strategy, and requires considerable innovation and often investment in order to implement the ideas.

Some potential new sources of income may not be "new" as such, but rather changes to existing sources. For example,

European funding may be made available for new qualifying areas of service, and hence become a new funding source; the government of the day often creates new areas of funding for specific services usually swayed by political priorities. In order to ensure that income is maximised from these types of funding source, the organisation needs to be up to date with all the current and planned future change being made by funding bodies, such that they can plan to exploit any opportunities when they arise. Allied to this, organisations can actively lobby for particular types of funding and, therefore, create a new source of funding in the process.

Other potential new sources of income can arise from:

- ❖ Developing new service areas for which charges can be made (e.g. internet café's in the lobby area)

- ❖ Introducing charges for existing services that were previously free (e.g. certain types of advice and information, use of certain facilities, etc.)

- ❖ Approaching new grant giving organisations to fund innovative but relevant projects (e.g. developing a training programme for people with disabilities may attract funding from organisations which fund disability projects)

- ❖ Selling assets (although this is a short term strategy and must be carefully considered, as once an income generating asset is disposed of, future income streams are lost forever)

- ❖ Partnerships and joint ventures whereby synergy is possible, and everyone benefits including the public sector organisation

Using Third Parties

The public sector can also consider using third parties who undertake certain activities for which the organisation receives an income. This could be in the form of a share of the profits, an annual fee, or a monthly percentage of the turnover generated. For example, in exchange for a monthly fee, a local authority may award a recycling contract to a company to undertake all the authority's recycling. The contract may be awarded as a result of a tendering process that delivers the highest net income to the authority.

Other areas where third parties can be strategically used to generate income are:

- Service delivery intermediaries (delivering services on behalf of the public sector organisation)
- Debt collectors (debts may even be factored to agencies whose specialist business is debt recovery)
- Marketing agencies (whose business is to promote services and to increase income)
- Fundraisers (who specialise in raising funds from a range of sources)

Using such third parties to generate income, is still a new concept for many public sector organisations, and some managers may find it difficult to reconcile a more commercial approach to income generation with the historic norms.

Investing to Generate Income

Many of the ideas already suggested will require some investment in order to realise the potential income. For example, the development of a new service area or project, will require initial investment in planning and implementation before any income is generated. In some cases, grant givers do fund this stage of a project, but this is not always the case.

Although it would seem an obvious strategy to invest in activities that will ultimately generate an income, it is not necessarily popular with the public sector as it carries with it a high element of risk. Public sector organisations are not in the business of taking risks, therefore, any such strategy must be extremely prudent, with the resulting income arising from the investment virtually guaranteed.

The other aspect of investing to generate income are the timescales. It is not unusual for the private sector to look at such strategies over a 5 to 10 year period, and not expect income streams to really be generated until this time. Public sector organisations, given the political environment in which they operate, are unlikely to wait as long to achieve favourable returns on its investment. However, the important approach is to properly analyse the cost and benefit of such income generating strategies and identify whether they are realistic.

One way of reducing the risk of investing to generate income, is to create business structures such as a "local authority company". A local authority company is one where the local authority has a majority shareholding interest, and can, therefore, influence the company's activities. As with any limited company, there is "limited liability" for the shareholders.

Utilising Spare Capacity

This is something that should be done as part of the routine of maximising existing sources of income, but it warrants a separate mention because many public sector organisations do not necessarily recognise where spare capacity exists. As the public sector has been striving towards achieving the 3Es, Effeciency, Effectiveness and Economy, many organisations feel under resourced and, therefore, do not recognise the spare capacity that may exist.

Spare capacity may take the form of:

- Office space and other buildings not being used, or which are under-utilised
- Land space not being used
- Non productive staff time
- Equipment and vehicles left idle for the majority of the time

Not all spare capacity can be income generating, but some can. Organisations should review all the areas of spare capacity that currently exist and develop appropriate strategies to eliminate it. For example:

Buildings:
An organisation may have many unoccupied areas in their buildings, which if they were to relocate staff, could free up a complete office floor or entire office building. The free space or property could then be let or sold to generate income. Some buildings within the organisation's property portfolios are suitable for evening and weekend lettings and, therefore, research could be undertaken to identify whether the income generated from lettings during this time, would more than cover the cost of extending the opening hours.

Land:

Public sector organisations often have land that is not being utilised, or where plans for development have never been implemented due to lack of funds or planning difficulties. Land is a valuable resource, and the organisation should consider sale or leasing as possible options taking into account any restrictions which may exist. Depending on where the land is located, it may at least be hired out for activities such as fairs, boot sales, and so on.

Staff time:

This is a more difficult area as it is not possible to expect a member of staff with an idle hour to suddenly switch to an activity which may be income generating. It is possible, however, to identify posts which seem to have times when they are not fully utilised and consider how those posts are filled. This would include the use of part-time and temporary staff, hence potentially reducing staff costs. It may also be possible to re-organise staff in order to free up a usable block of time that could be used for other, perhaps income generating activities.

Equipment and Vehicles:

There is potential for idle equipment and vehicles to be hired depending on the asset, or sold if it is no longer appropriate for the organisation. There is often a market for second hand equipment here and overseas, especially in countries where there are scarcities of such items. Obsolete equipment and vehicles should also be removed as soon as possible, as it incurs costs with relation to storage, and in some cases continued maintenance.

Fundraising

Public sector organisations can undertake their own fundraising initiatives and many have been very successful in this regard; hospitals have raised funds to purchase major items of equipment; schools have raised funds to install swimming pools; and nursing homes have raised funds to purchase mini buses.

Fundraising can take many forms including:

> **Events**
> (individuals, groups, corporate or community, e.g. street parties)
>
> **Sponsorships**
> (individual or corporate)
>
> **Gifts and donations**
> (individual or corporate)
>
> **Legacies**
> (individual)

Some people consider that the public sector should not have to undertake fundraising as an income generating strategy, as public services should be sufficiently well funded to meet all their basic requirements in the first instance. Fundraising is, therefore, usually seen as providing for "extras". However, for some organisations this is not the case, and fundraising needs to be viewed as integral to the overall financial strategy. The effectiveness of fundraising activities can vary dramatically, and as with many other income generation strategies, there will be some investment required. For example, organising a simple "fun run" will invariably require some initial expenditure.

Fundraising tends to be most effective if:

- It relates to a specific item, i.e. not just for general running expenses

- There is a target amount of income required, such that there is a success factor when the target is reached or exceeded
- It attracts wide ranging publicity and support, particularly from the local community
- There is public recognition of those who take part in fundraising activities
- It is professionally organised and co-ordinated

As already mentioned, raising income will often have an associated cost and the organisation must always consider the cost relative to the expected additional income stream. In some cases it is worthwhile undertaking a cost benefit analysis exercise to ensure that the risk of ending up in a net expenditure position, as a result of trying to maximise income, is minimised.

Summary

- Public sector organisations need to have in place strategies that enable them to maximise their income in all areas

- Basic systems are necessary to ensure grants are properly applied for, billing and collection of fees and charges are accurate, timely and complete, and services are delivered to the appropriate quality standards

- In some public sector organisations, existing customers can be a source of additional income, e.g. they can be a captive market for product or service sales, additional charges and fee increases, fundraising and so on

- Where possible, new sources of income should be sought at every opportunity. This will require creative and innovative approaches to service delivery and identification of where public services can be "commercialised" or "grant aided"

- Many organisations could review their spare capacity in all areas, and may identify ways in which this can be used to generate income

- Public sector organisations, as well as the voluntary sector, sometimes require a fundraising strategy over and above their existing funding sources. There are many successful models of fundraising initiatives that have proved very beneficial for the of purchase new equipment, funding projects, and so on

Strategic Financial Planning for Public Sector Services

Exercise 5

Raising Income

A local authority under 5's service has 5 day nurseries, all of which have places for 50 children and their own building with outdoor play space. Fees are currently charged at £500 per month, although at least 50% of places are subsidised (some up to 100%). After an extensive service review, it was decided that this service should be self financing from next year onwards. This now means the service manager has the following financial objective:

"To raise a further £250,000 per annum from next year to extinguish the currently forecast deficit, based on current financial arrangements"

Listed below are a number of strategic options that have been put forward with respect to meeting the financial objective.

(a) **Give a list of the positive and negative aspects of each of the options**

	Options	Positive Aspects	Negative Aspects
A	Increase fees by £50 per month		
B	Introduce uniforms and charge for them. This should yield a net contribution of £100 per uniform		

Strategic Financial Planning for Public Sector Services

	Options	Positive Aspects	Negative Aspects
C	Sell advertising space in the monthly nurseries newsletter that goes to all parents and other subscribers. Expected earnings £5000 per month		
D	Hire rooms in the buildings in the evenings and at weekends to local groups. Assumed potential income of £500 per week for 40 weeks for each nursery, but there will be a £10,000 annual cost of security and administration per nursery		
E	Gain sponsorships and donations from local companies, and undertake fundraising events. This should yield £50,000 depending on effort (Each nursery's target would be £10,000 per year)		

Options		Positive Aspects	Negative Aspects
F	Issue a 10 year franchise for one nursery to be operated by the private sector with a levy of 15% of fees collected and nomination rights to 50% of places for two years. (Assume fees are increased to £600 per month.)		

(b) Circle below one or more of the options that you would most favour in order to meet the financial objective, and give the reasons for your choice

Options	A	B	C	D	E	F	Total Income Generated £.................

Reasons for Choice

Suggested solution on page 131

Exercise 6

Are you maximising your income?

List the ways in which you intend to maximise your income for each of the following areas (where relevant)

Income Source	Maximisation Strategy
Grants ⇨ ⇨ ⇨ ⇨	
Sales ⇨ ⇨ ⇨ ⇨	
Fees ⇨ ⇨ ⇨ ⇨	
Charges ⇨ ⇨ ⇨ ⇨	

Strategic Financial Planning for Public Sector Services

Income Source	Maximisation Strategy
Rent ⇨ ⇨ ⇨ ⇨	
Interest ⇨ ⇨ ⇨ ⇨	
Capital Receipts (sale of capital assets) ⇨ ⇨ ⇨ ⇨	

Chapter 5

COST BENEFIT ANALYSIS

Strategic financial planning requires an organisation to make financial decisions which will affect it now and in the future. This is particularly the case with respect to investment decisions and the way in which future services are to be delivered. Cost benefit analysis can be used as a strategic planning tool to assist in this decision making process. It will not only assist in the decision making with respect to a single project, activity or investment, but can also be used to assess comparative projects which is particularly useful in an "either or situation".

Cost benefit analysis can be performed with minimal calculations, using a purely broad brush consideration of the costs and benefits involved. Conversely, it can be performed more objectively using mathematical calculations including net present values, probabilities and so on. However, given the political and social environment in which the public sector operates, this type of analysis will invariably need to take account of costs and benefits that are intangible in nature.

In the following paragraphs we examine:

❖   *Establishing costs and benefits*

❖   *Measuring intangible costs and benefits*

❖   *Undertaking the cost benefit analysis*

❖   *Public versus Private Sector Service delivery*

Establishing Costs and Benefits

Costs and Benefits can be broadly divided into two categories, tangible and intangible.

Tangible costs and benefits can easily be valued in monetary terms, whereas the intangibles are far more difficult to quantify and attribute a monetary value to. However, in order to undertake any meaningful cost benefit exercise, it is necessary to consider both types of costs in a way that is measurable and, therefore, comparable. The different types of costs and benefits which are usually measured include:

	Tangible	Intangible
Costs	• Land and Buildings • Development and Refurbishment • Machinery, Equipment, Furniture etc. • Employees • Materials • Contractors • Overheads • Interest, etc	• Opportunity cost • Increased risk • Low morale • Poor quality service • High level of complaints • Poor public perception
Benefits	• Increased income • Savings • Reduced revenue expenditure • Waste reduction • Reduced complaints • Increased efficiency	• High morale • Reduced sickness levels • Increased quality • Increased satisfaction levels • Political advantage • Raising the profile • Reduced risk

The tangible costs and benefits are easily identified using the following example:

A local authority manager is responsible for implementing a financial plan for the training unit, which includes the purchase of a building to become a central training centre, not just for the local authority, but also for all the area's public and voluntary organisations. The investment in the centre should create an economy of scale and synergy from which everyone can benefit. The building will be owned by the local authority and rooms rented to the other parties. The plan will be that the income generated from the building and training courses, will enable the unit to be self sufficient, and hence operate with a zero budget. This will result in a saving of £200,000 per annum for the local authority, which represents the current net expenditure budget for the unit.

The cost of the building with refurbishment is £350,000, fittings and equipment total a further £250,000. Although the project has general support from the executive board, the manager has still been asked to justify the investment in the project with a detailed cost benefit analysis. Not having previously undertaken a similar exercise, the manager decided to take the following factors into account:

Capital Costs
    Building and Refurbishment   £600,000 initial outlay
    Project Management   £100,000 initial outlay
        700,000

Annual Revenue Expenditure
    Annual running costs (of building) £200,000 per annum
    Management of the training unit £100,000 per annum
    * Cost of capital (5% per annum) £35,000 per annum
        £335,000

Annual revenue income benefits
    Net income from in-house training £150,000 per annum
    Rental charges to other organisations £125,000 per annum
    Savings on room hire £60,000 per annum
        £335,000

Savings on previous budget £200,000 per annum

*   interest on the Capital Costs (i.e. £700,000 x 5%)

The figures were based on the assumptions that the building work would be completed within a year, and that the 10 room building would be fully utilised with at least 50% of the rooms being let for 250 days per annum, at £100 per day.

On the basis of the above actual tangible costs, the manager presented the following report.

There is a need to raise an initial investment of £700,000, but thereafter, there would be a net benefit of £200,000 per year, which would mean that after three and a half years, the cost would have been fully extinguished with ongoing annual savings. Hence, it is clear that the benefits over time exceed the cost, and it is a strategically sound financial plan with real long term financial benefits.

A cost benefit analysis calculation can assist with a whole range of financial decisions, not just if to make a capital investment. It is useful in deciding on whether to:

- deliver a service
- close down a service
- gain quality standards
- train and develop staff
- invest in marketing
- invest in technology

Cost benefit analysis can also be useful in helping to address the question, "what is the cost of not performing?" For example, from the above list, the cost of not delivering the service may be compensation payments to clients who have not received their entitlements; the cost of not closing down a service may be the inability to deliver another more important service; and the cost of not gaining a quality standard may mean the loss of a contract or the inability to bid for certain contracts.

One of the difficulties in assessing costs and benefits, is measuring the intangibles. Many people, including finance staff, dislike dealing with issues which cannot be properly quantified. However, service managers often take more account of the intangible rather than the tangible issues. For example, the quality of a service is of key importance to a service manager, but a finance manager would wish to know how could that quality be converted into a measurable entity to which monetary values, such as unit costs, can be attached.

Measuring Intangible Costs and Benefits

The key to valuing intangible costs and benefits is to begin with a definition of what they are. Using the intangible costs and benefits shown in the table on page 86, we consider how best to define and establish a monetary value for each.

Opportunity cost	This is the cost of <u>not</u> using the funds currently invested in a project, in an alternative way. This may be in an alternative project, or even just leaving the cash on deposit. For example, the opportunity cost of investing £500,000 in a project could be the interest lost on those funds had they been placed on bank deposit at the ruling interest rates, say 6%. This represents £30,000 a year.
Risk	The risk or increased risk of an investment decision should be firstly identified and specified. It can then be assessed by conducting the risk assessment approaches discussed in chapter 2. The actual cost of the risk may be the cost of insuring against the risk, or the cost of the actions needed to prevent or reduce the risks in question.

Low morale	This may arise if the investment decision or action to be taken is not what was wanted by staff. This may include the closure of a service or premises, or the contracting out of a service. These decisions may be strategically sound for the benefit of the organisation, but may have a negative impact on staff, particularly in the short term until an adjustment is made to the new service arrangements. This will have a cost which could be measured in reduced productivity, increased absences, increased use of temporary or agency staff, and so on. In order to undertake an appropriate calculation of the cost, considerable monitoring needs to take place such that a judgement about future costs can be made using the historic results of similar actions.
Poor quality service	Sometimes there is a direct cost with respect to correcting errors, or repeating the service. These costs can be measured if adequate monitoring systems are in place. However, other costs are very difficult to measure such as customer complaints, poor image, loss of reputation, etc.
High levels of complaints	As mentioned above quality might be one area of complaint but there are many other things that result in complaints such as rude staff, waiting times, untidy or dirty surroundings, changes in services, etc. Most organisations have a complaints procedure which has to be followed and can often take up a lot of staff time. This obviously has a cost and can be measured if the organisation analyses and monitors staff time.
Poor public perception	Again this may be linked to poor quality services, but perceptions are not necessarily developed as a result of this. It may be that the organisation has a poor public image or has had some negative publicity about a one off incident that tarnishes the whole service. A poor public perception tends to make people complain more, show a negative attitude to the organisation, reluctance to volunteer, and stop using some facilities which may be income generating.
High morale	In contrast to low morale, this is an intangible benefit that can arise from staff being happy with the decision made. The same approach to measurement needs to take place as described above, i.e. the impact of increased productivity, reduced absence, etc.

Reduced sickness levels	This benefit may result from high morale or better working conditions. For example, an investment in better equipment may make a task less stressful or less difficult and hence, has a direct impact on the number of sick days taken. By undertaking a unit costing exercise, the cost per sick day can be calculated and used to put a value on sickness levels (reductions and increases).
Increased quality	This can be a very intangible area if the service or activity has not clearly defined what quality means. Ideally quality should be stated in specific terms such as waiting times, response rates, complaints, customer satisfaction, and so on. If this is done, then unit costing exercises can identify the cost per complaint, the cost per customer seen, the cost per letter sent, and so on. These costs can then be used to assess quality. Some areas of service would state that quality is about how clients feel, or prevention measures. These areas can still be defined and assessed. For example, if an investment is made in a project to prevent vandalism, the cost of vandalism can be calculated and the benefit will be the reduction in that cost. Similarly if quality is making people happy, this can be given an assumed cost based in terms of the cost of people being unhappy and complaining. Levels of "happiness" can be gained by undertaking surveys, etc and asking clients the appropriate questions.
Increased satisfaction levels	As for quality, the benefit of satisfaction can be measured by considering the cost of dis-satisfaction.
Political advantage	This benefit may be difficult to measure without a definition of what political advantage means. For example, it may mean more votes, in which case a value needs to be attached to each vote.

Raising the profile	This can be worth a great deal of money in the private sector, where the profile can often dictate the amount that can be charged for products. In the public sector, profile is becoming more important. It can affect an organisation's success in bidding for funding, and the way in which the public respond to various initiatives promoted by the organisation. A high and positive profile can be reflected in tangible income received. In order to assess the benefit in a cost benefit analysis calculation, the profile should be directly related to the project under review, and the impact on that particular project should be calculated using sound assumptions.
Reduced risk	The benefit should be reflected in the savings on the cost of risk, as considered above. It may also be considered in relation to a specific project. For example, if the project focussed on health and safety, there would be a direct benefit with respect to the reduced risk to health, and the savings resulting from reduced accidents at work, or reduced sickness absence, and so on.

Undertaking the Cost Benefit Analysis

Having established all the costs and benefits relating to a spending decision, the cost benefit calculation can be made more accurate by incorporating the following mathematical techniques:

Present values:

This technique provides a value of future income or expenditure at today's prices. These values will vary depending on the discount factor selected. This discount rate will usually reflect the expected average inflation rate over the future period. If comparative exercises are to be undertaken, it is important to ensure the discount rates used are consistent. Cost benefit analysis often incorporates looking at costs incurred today which yield benefits in the future. The value of the future benefits is more accurately compared with the costs if they are stated in today's monetary terms.

Probabilities:

This technique incorporates the concept of certainty and uncertainty into the cost benefit analysis, and is particularly useful when trying to assess the impact of risk. Probabilities relate to expected outcomes, some of which are more likely than others. Probabilities range from 0 (impossibility that the outcome will occur), to 1 (100% certainty that the outcome will occur). For example, the outcome when you toss a coin is certain insofar as it is either going to be heads or tails. The probability of the outcome of heads is the same as the probability of the outcome of tails, hence, there is a 0.5 (50%) probability of heads, and a 0.5 (50%) probability of tails. The probability of it being either heads or tails is 1, as one of those outcomes is certain to occur, and the probability of it being neither heads nor tails is 0, i.e. impossibility.

Following on from the training unit example on page 87:

> Having reviewed the report from the manager with respect to the cost benefit analysis for the training centre investment, the executive board decided to have it re-examined by a consultant before the final decision was taken. The consultant identified the following weaknesses with the existing calculations:

a) There was no risk assessment on the assumptions

b) There was no adjustment of any of the future income or expenditure cash flows for present day values

c) There was no account taken of any intangible costs or benefits

Based on their experience, the consultants made the following additional assumptions:

There would be a 70% probability of the project overrunning by 3 months, incurring additional costs in the form of lost income and additional interest. A contingency for the overrun should be made and was calculated as £102,200.

The probability of letting all the rooms for 250 days a year was 80%, and hence income should reflect the shortfall in lettings and be reduced to £100,000.

There is an intangible opportunity cost of using the capital elsewhere, and this should be reflected in the cost of capital. A reasonable assumption would change this from 5% used by the manager to 7%.

There are intangible benefits that can be taken into account, such as higher productivity as a result of the training courses. Net income from in-house training should, therefore, be increased by 10% to £165,000.

The consultants advised that the corporate financial strategy should evaluate projects over a 5 year period to assess their viability. They decided to use this period to determine the present values of the income and expenditure, in this case using a discount factor of 5%.

Initial outlay costs:		Present Values:
Building, refurbishment, project management	£700,000	
Contingency for overrun	£102,200	
Total		£802,200

Net Annual Benefit for 5 years:

Income:		
Training and room hire (165,000 + 100,000)	£265,000	
Savings on budget and room hire	£260,000	
Less: Expenditure:		
Management and running cost	£300,000	
*Cost of capital (7%)	£49,000	
Net Income	£176,000	

*interest on capital costs (i.e. £700,000 x 7%).

Present Value of £176,000 @ 5% for 5 years

Year	Discount Factor 5%	Present Value
1	0.9524	167,622
2	0.9070	159,632
3	0.8638	152,029
4	0.8227	144,795
5	0.7835	137,896
Total		£761,974

Comparing the two figures shows that the cost of £802,200, exceeds the expected value of the net benefit of £761,974 over a 5 year period, however, the contingency of £102,200, if removed, would make it a positive outcome and a viable project. The consultants recommended to proceed with the project with prudence and caution, stressing the importance of ensuring the project was completed on time.

The result of the consultant's analysis above, shows the project is not as clear cut as originally indicated by the manager. Clearly, it highlights the potential for making poor long term strategic financial decisions, based on insufficient information and analysis.

Public versus Private Sector Service Delivery

One of the financial decisions that may need to be made by many public sector organisations is whether or not to contract out all or part of the service to the private sector. Again this is a decision that can be assisted by looking at the costs and benefits associated with contracting out services. Each individual case will be different, but all may benefit from the completion of a cost benefit analysis matrix which will enable the decision making team to consider whether contracting out will deliver best value services in the long term. In the following table, a comparison is made of the tangible and intangible costs and benefits to be experienced by the organisation when the service is provided by the public sector in-house team, compared to that provided by a private sector organisation.

	Public/in-house service provision	Private sector service provision
COSTS		
Tangible	• Property • Equipment • Vehicles • Employees • Supplies and services • Capital charges • Other revenue expenses • Complaints • Waste/under utilisation	• Contractor payments • Variation orders • Contract development and preparation • Contract management • Complaints
Intangible	• Quality • Customer satisfaction • Staff motivation • Risk management • Opportunity cost	• Opportunity cost • Reduced control • Reduced flexibility

Strategic Financial Planning for Public Sector Services

	Public/in-house service provision	**Private sector service provision**
BENEFITS		
Tangible	• Potential fees/income generation • Potential for savings • Access to grants and other third party funding • Fundraising • Appreciation of property values • Customer satisfaction	• Potential for savings – not always the case • Potential for net contributions depending on the service • Reduction in risk • Potential for service improvement • Potential for capital investment • Potential for investment in technology, equipment and so on • Customer service
Intangible	• Control over service delivery • Flexibility • Customer contact and relationships • Responsiveness to customer need • Knowledge and Experience	• Potential for future investment • Research and development • Greater innovation • More up to date technology • Access to international experience and expertise

The same approach can be given to other models of service delivery, such as whether to undertake partnership arrangements, joint ventures, raise private finance through the Private Finance Initiative, and so on. Cost benefit analysis is a useful tool when making strategic financial decisions, and it should be part of the overall decision making approach.

Summary

- Cost benefit analysis is a useful tool in making strategic financial decisions that will have a long term impact on the organisation

- The full costs and benefits need to be established by considering both the tangible and intangible cost and benefits of a project or proposed activity

- Cost benefit analysis calculations can be applied to capital and revenue investment decisions

- Where possible, intangible costs and benefits need to be stated in financial terms

- Mathematical tools such as calculating present values and using probabilities, can assist in obtaining a more realistic and accurate cost benefit analysis calculation

- When assessing whether or not to have private sector in in-house service delivery, completing a cost benefit analysis matrix may assist with the financial decision making

Exercise 7

Public versus private sector

You are responsible for the delivery of services for older people, and currently have 4 residential homes under your control. There have been a number of problems with the homes and the director of service has decided that they may be better served by allowing a private or voluntary sector organisation take over. The decision is to be made on the basis of a financial case, and to assist with the decision making, a cost benefit analysis is to be undertaken. In order to produce the analysis, the following financial information has been provided.

	The Anvil	Boston House	Cronvale	Dingle Lodge
Bedspaces	40	24	12	24
Cost per bed per year	£12,000	£13,000	£10,000	£11,000
Benchmark cost per bed	£10,000	£10,000	£10,000	£10,000
Fees (£13,000 per bed)	£416,000	£219,000	£156,000	£249,000
Expenditure	£480,000	£312,000	£120,000	£264,000
Surplus/Deficit(-)	£-64,000	£-93,000	£36,000	£-15,000
Investment required to meet standards	£100,000	£150,000	£50,000	£100,000
Property Value	£500,000	£350,000	£200,000	£450,000
Private Sector Bid	£200,000	NIL	£300,000	£200,000

Occupancy rates vary, but average at approximately 90% across all four sites, and bad debts are currently running on average at 10%.

The private sector is only interested in the service as a whole, i.e. all four sites, and is not interested in taking individual packages, even though individual bids have been sent out.

The organisation evaluates projects over a 5 year period using a discount factor of 5%.

Using the above information, undertake a cost benefit analysis and determine whether or not there will be a net benefit in selling the service to the private sector. (Present Value Tables on page 136)

Suggested solutions on page 134.

Exercise 8

Cost Benefit Analysis in Practice

Take a project with which you have been involved, and complete the following cost benefit matrix. It does not matter whether the project is yet to start or is something that is already in progress.

Using the matrix and attaching as many figures to each area as possible, assess whether or not the project is really producing a net benefit to the organisation.

	Tangible	Intangible
Costs		
Benefits		

Chapter 6

ALTERNATIVE FINANCIAL STRATEGIES CONSIDERED

This chapter sets out examples of a number of financial strategies and considers their impact on the organisation's financial resources with respect to income, expenditure, unit costs, Best Value, and long term financial viability. The strategies are not mutually exclusive, and one or more could be adopted at any one time. The important issue is that public sector organisations do not pursue financial strategies that lead to a spend and cuts culture, or a stop and go approach to service delivery and development. The aim should be to implement strategies that promote continuous organisational development, even in a climate where resource may be diminishing. Effective financial planning with clear objectives and strategies should take account of not just the current financial environment in which the organisation operates, but should also consider the financial environment of the future.

These examples represent a mixture of activities used in a variety of public sector organisations, many of which did not have one clear financial strategy in mind.

Devolvement, Business Units and Bank Accounts

The Objective:

To make managers more accountable and responsible for the finances and as such, deliver services that are more efficient, effective and economic which directly meet the needs of the community.

The strategy:

- ❖ Devolve all aspects of financial planning and control for service delivery to the lowest possible level of management.

- ❖ Develop practical business units that reflect service delivery in the devolved structure, and which are run autonomously.

- ❖ Provide support services through self-financing business units that will only survive on a commercial basis.

- ❖ Reduce central service support to a minimum, reducing the burden of overheads on services and redistributing some of the resources accordingly.

- ❖ Targets for savings and performance to be developed at a local level and fed upwards such that strategic financial decisions can be made.

- ❖ Business units to be able to bid for allocations from the capital programme subject to existing projects being completed.

- ❖ Internal audit to be part of the Chief Executives department, and strengthened to take account of the greater need for checks and balances to ensure financial probity and protect against fraud.

The Implementation:

- ☞ Training given to all staff with respect to their new roles and responsibilities
- ☞ Financial regulations, management and control manuals written and distributed to managers
- ☞ Bank accounts set up with a central account for treasury management
- ☞ New computer systems put in place, which were user friendly and could be tailored to meet local needs
- ☞ Internal invoicing and recharging system set up for the support service trading units
- ☞ Consultants engaged to assist managers, trouble shoot, and monitor the progress of the transition
- ☞ Performance management appraisal system, clear targets set and penalties for non performance
- ☞ All staffing grades reviewed to reflect new responsibilities

The Results:

The short term results were very patchy, with certain departments very resistant to the change and wanting to retain a more centralised approach to financial control. There was also resistance from some managers with respect to undertaking the new role, although the re-grading did help to encourage some managers to make the transition quickly. The level of overspends were in the same areas, and of the same order as in previous years, although there was a seed change in attitude which was encouraging.

At least three areas of support service proved unviable. This was due to the size of the unit, and the management expertise which lacked entrepreneurial flair and a knowledge of marketing and pricing. The units were supported in the first year even though they were loss making, and with a change in management, two of the units were able to break even in the second year. Unfortunately, the marketing and design unit had to close resulting in a number of redundancies.

Operating bank accounts proved to be very difficult and produced more administrative work, particularly in the area of writing cheques and reconciling bank statements. Interestingly though, this was one of the areas, which in a staff survery, a high percentage of managers considered to be an improvement. They felt more in control of their financial resources, and were more careful in the way they spent the organisation's funds as they had to sign the cheques. They also found that they were more efficient in paying suppliers and contractors than under the old central system.

After three years, there was a considerable change in some of the departments which achieved increased efficiency, service quality, customer satisfaction along with savings on their budget. However, there was still one department which did not show any signs of improvement, and the management were not properly implementing the devolved structure. Clearly, the financial model was sound, but the commitment of management to change was not. Therefore, although progress was certainly made, the total benefit has not yet been reaped, and a change in management may be the solution.

Outsourcing, Tendering and Contracting

The objective:

To become an enabler of service provision rather than a provider, and to maximise the use of financial resources by effective procurement from third parties

The strategy

- ❖ To review all service areas and re-organise into practical business units which could be outsourced or tendered at some stage

- ❖ Business units to be autonomous and accountable for their income and expenditure on a commercial basis. Budgets should be viewed as income and over and underspends would be carried forward from year to year

- ❖ To undertake market testing on each business unit, to identify if there is a market place and the attractiveness of the service provision to third parties or potential partners

- ❖ To create a market place in areas of service where markets do not already exist, by offering inducements to the private and voluntary sectors to enter the market, and packaging services in a way that would be attractive to organisations with the relevant ability to deliver the service

- ❖ Encourage current in-house providers to bid for their own services either as independent bodies, i.e. forming companies with backers in a management buyout, or in partnership with the private sector

- ❖ Develop expertise in contracting, contract management, and service specification

- ❖ Develop a team focussing on customer complaints, customer satisfaction, and external communications

- ❖ Develop training courses which will equip managers to either compete for their service, or become part of an external provider's organisation

- ❖ Ensure that the total cost of letting the contract, and the contract value itself, results in a saving on the current cost of service provision, or ensure a higher service quality specification for the same price as the current cost of service provision

- ❖ Undertake benchmarking exercises to evaluate the true costs of services provided by existing business units, and the ball-park contract price that should be expected from bidders

- ❖ Establish a programme which outsources elements of service provision, including support services, or tenders them on the open market

- ❖ Retained services that cannot be outsourced or tendered due to legal restrictions or practicality, will continue to operate on a business unit basis with a view to seeking public sector partnership where possible

The Implementation:

- ☞ Training given to all staff with respect to management skills, entrepreneurship, business units, and so on.

- ☞ Business units were developed initially along the lines of cost centres and then merged to become practical sized units

- ☞ Consultants engaged to assist with market testing, market development, benchmarking and establishing a contract management team

- ☞ Consultants engaged to assist business unit managers, and contract managers, to develop specifications for tendering

- Preferred suppliers lists developed for all kinds of goods and services, and more effective procurement arrangements made achieving greater discounts
- Some areas of services outsourced with existing external providers whose contracts were amended accordingly
- A rolling programme of tendering business units
- A central contract management division created with expertise in service specification, developing contracts, and monitoring contracts and contractors

The Results:

This radical approach to service provision through contracting was viewed with sceptism at all levels in the organisation. Staff were particularly anxious that they would be working for different employers; most would be transferred under TUPE (Transfer of Undertakings, Protection of Employment) rules. Some tenders were unsuccessful, leading staff to be in a state of flux for many months, not knowing when re-tendering was to take place, if at all.

Significant savings were realised on some contracts, particularly in areas where there was a buoyant market place such as the support services (legal, audit, training, personnel, recruitment, etc.). Other contracts achieved very little saving, with potential to be more expensive if they had to be varied in any way. Another problem arose with respect to specifying services. Specifications tended to be developed on existing needs and did not take account of the organisation's future needs. Many of the contracts were let for five or more years, and during that time, changes to the contracts to meet the organisation's needs proved costly.

Service quality improved in some areas and worsened in others. Cleaning contracts performed particularily badly, with one of the contractors folding before the end of the contract term. The communications team proved to be a great success, with the public feeling they can communicate with the organisation easily with high levels of responsiveness, especially to complaints.

Overall, there was a significant learning curve to go through, particularly with respect to specifying services correctly, developing contracts with adequate penalties and incentives, effective monitoring of contracts, and working with third party contractors. However, after 5 years the strategy is still being continued and the underperforming contracts relet. Management now focus on long term planning, looking strategically at service development, customer needs and requirements. The strategy has continued as although the same contracts have proved more expensive than in-house provision, on balance there has been significant savings, allowing more funds to be invested in direct service delivery for the benefit of local people.

Providing More for Less

The objective:

To deliver more and better quality services with a reduced budget

The strategy:

- Develop training programmes for all staff at all grades which focus on ensuring staff know how to undertake their work, have a customer focus, understand productivity and its impact on unit costs and the budget

- Develop detailed quality manuals for every area of service

- Achieve quality kite marks such as Investors in People, ISO9000, and Charter Marks for all services

- Introduce non financial incentive schemes for staff, which encourages them to work harder. For example, employee of the month, plaques, shields, all expenses paid holiday for the employee of the year

- Create high morale amongst staff by having team building days, staff parties, lunchtime forums, staff surveys, suggestion boxes, staff welfare scheme, and so on

- Engage consultants to examine work flow issues in all service areas, and suggest how efficiency could be improved and waste minimised

- Set service improvement targets with staff, and incorporate these targets into individual workplans and the appraisal scheme

- Set savings targets for each service area where savings can be realistically achieved, and encourage an "invest to save" philosophy so that managers take a long term sustainable view to savings

The Implementation:

- Training given to all staff at every grade within the organisation
- Consultants engaged to assist service areas achieve quality kite marks
- In order to monitor productivity, timesheets introduced for all staff including managers
- New computer systems put in place which were user friendly and could be tailored to meet local needs, and enabled increased efficiency in a number of areas
- Increased monitoring of waste time and other resources
- Consultants engaged to assist managers produce quality manuals and achieve the most effective workflow within each service area
- A performance management appraisal system implemented with clear targets set and penalties for non performance
- All staff involved in the change process with the use of quality circles, motivation groups, quality monitoring teams, and employee of the year scheme (given a very high profile internally and externally)

The Results:

There was a desire to change the culture within the organisation, and staff relished the opportunity for involvement in the change process and becoming part of a team all working to the same goal. The simple goal of more for less, although requiring more effort from staff, was something all staff could relate to and accepted as a reality of the present day public sector.

In the first year, there was little change in productivity and no savings achieved, although areas of overspending reduced. In the second year, when the employee of the year scheme captured the imagination of all service areas and all staff, there was a significant increase in productivity which reflected itself in the need for less temporary staff, and higher staff retention rates. Both these factors lead to significant savings. Customer satisfaction ratings were higher and service quality in many areas improved, this was coupled with the achievement of IIP in some areas.

By year 3, the organisational culture had totally changed. There was openness, a great deal of communication between peers and with management. Time sheets are an accepted part of the routine of working and proper monitoring of productivity can now be achieved in all service areas. The results of the staff survey showed high levels of morale and commitment, and this has yielded tangible benefits in terms of savings as a result of reduced sickness levels, reduced waste, increased efficiency, and greater productivity.

Community Choice

The objective:

To involve the local community in the decision making with respect to how financial resources should be used, and to be totally accountable to the community for the financial management and control of those resources.

The strategy:

❖ Set up community forums in every local area which are open to the general public and use local papers, radio stations and bill boards to promote the idea of community choice and how people can become involved

❖ Invite community representatives to senior management and committee meetings so that they can communicate community views during decision making processes

❖ Provide an Internet site which enables local people to register their view points on a whole range of issues, and get involved in decisions which are put forward for the community vote

❖ Establish a community liaison team that has responsibility for ensuring the community really takes part in the decision making processes

❖ Issue monthly progress statements in the local newspaper, and send out a quarterly review document delivered door to door, which sets out the organisation's financial position, whether or not targets have been achieved, and the plans for the rest of the year and future years. A response mechanism should be part of this allowing local feedback

- ❖ Obtain sponsorship for Community Choice from other public and private organisations which may wish to use the initiative to promote their own organisations, or to collect data for their own use
- ❖ Identify critical success factors to ensure the objective is being fulfilled, such as ensuring the next major capital expenditure project is selected by the community from a range of options

The Implementation:

- ☞ A community liaison team established with the assistance of consultants to spearhead all the new community initiatives
- ☞ Community forums set up in schools, doctors surgeries, community centres, housing area offices, and libraries
- ☞ The health authority, police authority and the two main housing associations joined forces, with initiating the local authority to work together and open the scope of Community Choice to a wider range of issues and spending. This partnership enabled more resources to be placed into developing the community forums into real information exchange groups
- ☞ An Internet company sponsored the internet site and developed on line voting for local spending decisions with respect to particular projects
- ☞ Community Choice launched in a blaze of publicity and put in the spotlight nationally and internationally

The Results:

Although the large partnership created synergy, economies of scale, and increased the pool of resources, there was tension between the parties involved due to their differing objectives. The aim was to enable the community to have control of real money, and not just rubber stamp decisions made by officers of the public sector authority. Agreeing terms of reference delayed the progress of the intiative, resulting in little to show in the first year.

Eventually, it was agreed that Community Choice would dictate 25% of the local authority's capital expenditue budget, and the other authorities also put forward individual project choices for the community. The most impressive being the health authority who decided to let the community decide on the location, service delivery and opening hours of a new health centre.

The opportunity to be involved in local public sector spending was very exciting to a small minority of local people, the majority still did not take any interest and did not get involved at any level. The promotion techniques used were effective, because an independent high street survey showed that over 70% of people had heard of Community Choice and knew what it was about. The most common response with respect to why people were not participating was lack of time, a disbelief that their opinions would be listened to and general apathy.

Having established the community forums, they have proved a very useful network for consulting the public with respect to the Best Value regime. There is a fear that Community Choice will only reflect the wishes of the few and not the many, and hence may fall into disrepute.

Maximising Income, Minimising Costs, and Building Reserves

The objective:

To ensure that all forms of income are maximised and all forms of costs are minimised, such that surpluses are generated annually, and reserves can be developed to a level that secures long term viability and allows for a self financing capital programme.

The strategy:

- ❖ Every year increase all fees and charges by at least inflation, ideally slightly above the rate of inflation depending on the service area being affected

- ❖ Establish a grants unit with a focus on raising money from the UK, Europe and other international bodies. Their expertise will be grant applications and assisting managers with project development for grant funding

- ❖ Set income targets for all service areas that can generate income

- ❖ Create an effective marketing department to promote the organisation to grant funding bodies and other sponsors and donors

- ❖ Develop a policy which dictates that all purchases are at the lowest possible cost unless a strong case can be presented otherwise

- ❖ Revise terms and conditions of employment for all new staff to the lowest possible benefits with respect to sick pay, holidays, allowances and so on

❖ Eliminate all waste and underutilisation of time, and equipment by setting waste reduction targets for all service areas

❖ Reduce service delivery to minimum levels in most areas within the bounds of what is publicly acceptable

The Implementation:

☞ Fees and charges increased by 2% above inflation on average. Some fees had significantly higher rises than others, although all were increased

☞ Recruiting the correct calibre of staff to the proposed grants unit proved difficult, and in the short term a fundraising consultancy was engaged to undertake the remit of the grants unit until this could be established

☞ High income targets were set for all appropriate service areas, but financial forecasts were developed with a probability that only 75% of the income target would be reached

☞ Union representatives made an appeal with respect to changes in the terms and conditions of employment for new staff, which was negotiated until a compromise was reached. The new terms and conditions will retain some benefits such as the holiday levels, but will not have the same sickness allowances

☞ Reducing underutilisation of property resulted in a number of properties being emptied and sold, along with old and obsolete equipment

☞ The preferred suppliers list was reviewed and new suppliers encouraged to join, that would provide cheaper goods and services

☞ Some services were wound down in order to minimise service delivery and this resulted in redundancy costs and customer dis-satisfaction

☞ Performance management appraisal system implemented, with clear targets set in relation to the above strategies and penalties for non performance

The Results:

Income generation has increased over a three year period and has certainly been a large contributor the surpluses achieved over the last two years. Historically, this organisation had a history of small deficits each year. The objective has yielded quite dramatic results with costs falling in most areas. However, the other result has been to create an atmosphere of low morale due to service closures, changes in the terms and conditions for new staff, and the strict performance management appraisal system that has been implemented.

Senior management had always viewed this objective as a time limited one, until reserves had been built up to an acceptable level and a careful re-investment in service delivery could take place. This would enable management to be very strategic with respect to their financial plans for the future and ensure that financial resources were applied to areas of most need.

SOLUTIONS TO EXERCISES

Solutions to Exercises

Exercise 1
The Objectives 125

Exercise 3
Financial Decisions 127

Exercise 5
Raising Income 131

Exercise 7
Public versus Private Sector 134

Exercise 1
The Objectives

- Expenditure on all budgets to be reduced by 10% at today's levels through efficiency savings and economies of scale
- Generate income equivalent to 5% of the current budget from third parties, by selling spare capacity to other public and voluntary sector organisations
- Use income generated over three years to invest in upgraded computer systems and staff training
- Develop a contingency to target resources where they are most needed and to fund unforeseen peaks in workload
- Outsource any service unit that is unable to meet savings and income targets after three years, subject to cost benefit analysis

What financial strategies could Joanne adopt in order to achieve the objectives stated above?

Curtail the use of agency staff and recruit to vacant posts

Introduce measures to increase productivity of existing staff so as to require fewer posts

Set specific targets for Legal, Human Resources and Public Relations to generate the required level of income

Immediately outsource recruitment advertising and other elements of human resources that would yield savings

Devolve the responsibility and accountability for service area budgets to service centre managers, to monitor, control and set individual targets for savings and income

Market test all service areas to establish whether or not they are delivering value for money services

What level of contingency should be set given the current figures?

Some variances were one off occurrences and some could be rectified by making savings and generating income. On this basis the contingency could be set using those that are likely to re-occur, i.e. Central Finance, -80k, Legal, 10k, Human Resources, -170k, and Contract Management, -10k, giving a total of £250,000.

What are the key risk areas that should be considered and taken into account with respect to Joanne's financial objectives?

Income levels required may not be achieveable

Demand cannot be controlled, and hence spare capacity may not be available

Inflation rates

Cost of contracting out may be more than the savings achieved

Decreasing expenditure may result in reduced service quality

Strategic Financial Planning for Public Sector Services

Exercise 3

Financial Decisions

a)

Problem	Options
The capital programme is in trouble. One project with a value of £2.5m is delayed by 6 months and 3 projects are due to exceed budget by 10% totalling £1m	(a) Begin a substitute project and use the £2.5m within the timescale. Seek to raise the £1m overspend on 3 projects from sale of assets
	(b) Use £1m to fund the overspends on the 3 projects and identify another project to utilise £1.5m
	(c) Review the overspending budgets with a view to bringing expenditure back on track. If possible invest the £2.5m until project can be started

Decision

(b)
Most prudent option ensuring that the 3 projects can be completed, hence reducing risk.

This option will require new arrangements to be made for the original £2.5m project

b)

Problem	Options
Employees budget appears to be overspent by 10% due to the heavy dependence on temporary staff provided by agencies	(a) Renegotiate contract arrangements with agencies and force down rates otherwise do not use the agency
	(b) Recruit and fill vacancies, allow services to decline in the short term to generate savings
	(c) Establish an in-house bank of staff to cover absences and cease use of agency staff

Decision

(c)
Best decision for the long term to prevent overspends re-occurring

May have set up costs and may take time to put in place

c)

Problem	Options
Two properties have been put up for sale by auction and failed to meet their reserve prices (£300,000 each). They are both in a poor condition and require £250,000 investment in repairs. Doing nothing will result in the values declining and the cost of repair increasing	(a) Re-auction with a lower reserve price (b) Fund repairs by cutting an alternative capital project, undertake the repairs, and re-auction at a higher price (c) Seek partnership funding to undertake the repairs, and bring buildings temporarily back into use until property prices increase
Decision (c) If partners are available and if the properties can be utilised for service delivery, this will be the best long term decision as it will maximise income	

d)

Problem	Options
A major service area relating to a statutory responsibility of the organisation is overspent to date by £2million, on a budget of £12million for the year. Overspending in this area has been a major cause of the organisation's deficits for the last 3 years. The position has to be rectified	(a) Fund overspend from reserves and ensure budgets are set from a zero base from next year and truly reflect the necessary expenditure (b) Calculate expected outturn and total expected overspend for the year. Cut expenditure on other non statutory services to fund overspend. Revise content of service to minimum level for future years to reduce expenditure (c) Take personal responsibility for this budget and gain a real understanding of why budget overspends are occurring. Accept the reality of another deficit year, but ensure strong control introduced for the future
Decision (b) Real change has to take place if the deficits are to be reduced in the long term	

e)

Problem	Options
Outstanding debtors are currently £35million, which is £5million more than target. This has lead to an overdraft of £3million, which is the limit currently available to the organisation. The position appears to be deteriorating rather than improving	(a) Implement a stronger credit control and collection policy, outsourcing if necessary (b) Negotiate a new overdraft limit with existing bankers or change banks (c) Introduce incentives for advance payments, such as discounts, charge reductions, and so on

Decision

(a) and (c)
Combining these options allows for some immediate action coupled with changes that will provide a longer term increase in cash flows and reduction in debtors

f)

Problem	Options
A piece of land for which planning has been granted for the development of housing is to be sold, however the highest bidder is likely to be a private developer for luxury apartments and not the social housing sector, for which there is a great need in the area. A substantial profit on sale could be realised (up to £10million) depending on the selected purchaser	(a) Take the highest bidder in order to maximise profit and build reserves/fund overspends (b) Initiate a partnership between the private and social housing sector to allow for some social housing as part of the development, whilst maintaining a high bid price (c) Maximise bid price from the social housing sector even though profits may be lower, a significant contribution will still be obtained

Decision

(b)
Although this may not be income maximising, it would still be commercially sound and the intangible benefits of having some social housing may compensate for any lost profit on sale

g)

Problem	Options
The Director of Human Resources has identified a desperate need to train managers and consider it an essential part of the strategy to increase efficiency, service quality and performance. Central funding is being requested this year to pay consultants to develop the programme. The Xfile consultants require £250,000 to begin the project and were the only bidders	(a) Agree to the expenditure and fund it by using reserves or making expenditure savings in service areas (b) Insist on retendering with a repackaged specification to encourage more bidders, with a view to reducing the cost (c) Delay the whole programme to next year when provision for it can be made in next year's financial plan

Decision

(b) and (c)

Ideally there should be more than one bidder to ensure Best Value is being achieved, and expenditure should always be planned for in advance whenever possible

Strategic Financial Planning for Public Sector Services

Exercise 5

Raising Income

"To raise a further £250,000 per annum from next year onwards to extinguish the currently forecast deficit based on current financial arrangements"

(a) **Give a list of the positive and negative aspects of each of the options**

	Options	Income Generated	Positive Aspects	Negative Aspects
A	Increase fees by £50 per month	£150,000 (£50 per month x 50 children x 5 nurseries)	Immediate increase in income Easy target market to raise monies from	Existing parents are bound to be unhappy and dissatisfied New prices may be uncompetitive and hence it may be difficult to fill all the places
B	Introduce uniforms and charge for them. This should yield a net contribution of £100 per uniform	£25,000 (£100 per uniform x 50 children x 5 nurseries)	Tangible benefit to parents, and uniforms are often seen in a positive light Parents will tend to repeat purchase at least once per year	Cost may be too expensive for parents May not get a 100% take up, and hence a high level of risk attached
C	Sell advertising space in the monthly nurseries newsletter that goes to all parents and other subscribers. Expected earnings £5000 per month	£60,000 (£5000 x 12)	Income arising from external third parties May be able to develop a loyal customer base Potential to increase sales volumes and prices over time	May not reach sales targets, and therefore risk attached to advertising income figure Will require time and effort to get advertisers, which will be a hidden cost

	Options	Income Generated	Positive Aspects	Negative Aspects
D	Hire rooms in the buildings in the evenings and at weekends to local groups. Assumed potential income of £500 per week for 40 weeks for each nursery, but there will be a £10,000 cost of security and administration for each nursery for the year	£50,000 (£500 x 40 = £20,000 less £10,000 cost x 5 nurseries)	Good utilisation of property External income from third parties Increases links with the local community and may provide contacts for other income generating activities	May not get the level of demand required, and hence risk attached in the income Room rates may prove uncompetitive Increased risk of property damage with more users coming in and out of the buildings
E	Gain sponsorships, donations from local companies and undertake fundraising events. This should yield £50,000 depending on effort (Each nursery's target would be £10,000 per year)	£50,000	Income from external third parties without restriction on use Increases links with local community and businesses Raises profile of the nursery in the local area	Requires a lot of time and effort which is a hidden cost May be unsuccessful and, hence a high risk option Difficult to keep momentum going year on year
F	Issue a 10 year franchise for one nursery to be operated by the private sector with a levy of 15% of fees collected and nomination rights to 50% of places for two years. (Assume fees are increased to £600 per month.)	£54,000 (£600x12 x50x15%)	A regular invoice each year Less nurseries to manage No immediate disruption for half of the families in the short term	Half of the places will be lost leading to potential difficulties for parents Large fee increases for parents May be difficult to find an appropriate franchise

(b) Circle below one or more of the options that you would most favour in order to meet the financial objective and give the reason for your choice

Options	(A)	(B)	(C)	(D)	(E)	Total Income Generated £335,000

Reasons for Choice

A combination of all the above is required, as although the total amount is more than the requirement there is significant risk apparent in all the options, and hence the probability of obtaining the full amount from any one of them is likely to be less than 100%. Based on a probability of 80% success this would provide a total income of £268,000, marginally above the income requirement. (F) was not chosen because of the difficulties of franchising.

Exercise 7

Public versus Private Sector

First establish the total income and expenditure figures for all four sites.

	The Anvil £	Boston House £	Cronvale £	Dingle Lodge £	Total £
* Fees (£13,000 per bed)	416,000	219,000	156,000	249,000	1,040,000
Expenditure	480,000	312,000	120,000	264,000	1,176,000
Surplus/Deficit(-)	-64,000	-93,000	36,000	-15,000	-136,000
Investment required to meet standards	100,000	150,000	50,000	100,000	400,000
Property Value	500,000	350,000	200,000	450,000	1,500,000
Private Sector Bid	200,000	NIL	300,000	200,000	700,000

```
Check total fees                              £'000
Total Fees, 100 bed spaces @ £13,000          1,300
Less 10% for under occupancy                    130
Less 10% for bad debts                          130
Total net fees                                1,040
```

The costs and benefits with respect to accepting the private sector bid can be analysed as follows:

Costs		Benefits	
Loss of capital assets	£1,500,000	Income from bid	£ 700,000
Less: investment required	£ 400,000		
Total	£1,100,000	Savings from no longer having overspends of £136,000 per annum discounted over 5 years *	£ 588,798
		Total	£1,288,798

* Present value of £136,000 over 5 years, calculation is as follows:

Year	Discount Factor 5%	Present Value
1	0.9524	129,526
2	0.9070	123,352
3	0.8638	117,477
4	0.8227	111,887
5	0.7835	106,556
Total		588,798

The above analysis would indicate that the private sector bid yields a net benefit to the organisation

However, the cost benefit analysis does not take into account the intangible costs and benefits such as the service quality, staff morale, opportunity cost of losing an appreciating asset, utilisation of the cash inflow, and so on. It also assumes continuing overspends for the following five years, whereas it may have been possible to correct this position with efficiency savings, better cost control, etc.

The net benefit to the organisation as shown by the above calculation, is not of sufficient magnitude to make it a clear cut decision and other factors need to be taken into account before deciding whether or not to accept the private sector bid as it currently stands.

Strategic Financial Planning for Public Sector Services

Mathematical Tables

Present Value of £1 at the end of (n) periods

Period	Rate	1%	2%	3%	4%	5%	6%	7%	8%	9%	10%
1		.9901	.9804	.9709	.9615	.9524	.9434	.9346	.9259	.9174	.9091
2		.9803	.9612	.9426	.9246	.9070	.8900	.8734	.8573	.8417	.8264
3		.9706	.9423	.9151	.8890	.8638	.8396	.8163	.7938	.7722	.7513
4		.9610	.9238	.8885	.8548	.8227	.7621	.7629	.7350	.7084	.6830
5		.9515	.9057	.8626	.8219	.7835	.7473	.7130	.6806	.6499	.6209
6		.9420	.8880	.8375	.7903	.7462	.7050	.6663	.6302	.5963	.5645
7		.9327	.8706	.8131	.7599	.7107	.6651	.6227	.5835	.5470	.5132
8		.9235	.8535	.7894	.7307	.6768	.6274	.5820	.5403	.5019	.4665
9		.9143	.8368	.7664	.7026	.6446	.5919	.5439	.5002	.4604	.4241
10		.9053	.8203	.7441	.6756	.6139	.5584	.5083	.4632	.4224	.3855
11		.8693	.8043	.7224	.6496	.5847	.5268	.4751	.4289	.3875	.3505
12		.8874	.7885	.7014	.6246	.5568	.4970	.4440	.3971	.3555	.3186
13		.8787	.7730	.6810	.6006	.5303	.4688	.4150	.3677	.3262	.2897
14		.8700	.7579	6611	.5775	.5051	.4423	.3878	.3405	.2992	.2633
15		.8613	.7430	.6419	.5553	.4810	.4173	.3624	.3152	.2745	.2394

INDEX

Index

A

Action Plan 6
Agency Staff 47
Asset Management 57
Asset Risk 15
Assets 39, 56, 72

B

Bank Accounts 104
Best Value 6, 41, 96
Best Value Plan 5
Borrowing 42
Bottom Line 35
Budgets 10, 11
Building Reserves 117
Business Plan 6
Business Plan Objectives 38
Business Unit 6, 11, 107

C

Capital Expenditure 5, 42
Capital Investment 39
Cash Flow Forecast 10
Cash Flow 44
Cash Management 44
Central Government 31, 42, 68
Community Choice 114
Contingency Plan 21
Contracting 107
Contracting Out 33
Corporate Plan 5, 7
Cost Benefit Analysis 78, 92

Cost Centre 6, 11
Cost Minimisation 32
Cost of Service 52

D

Debt Collection 45
Departmental Business Plan 5, 6
Devolved Budgetary Responsibility 42
Devolvement 104

E

Economic Risk 14
Efficiency, Effectiveness, Economy 67, 75
European Funding 72

F

Fees and Charges 69
Financial Accounting Systems 54
Financial Control 3
Financial Decision Making 37
Financial Forecasting 10
   Cash Flow Forecast 10
   Income and Expenditure 10
Financial Management 30, 37
Financial Management Systems 54
Financial Monitoring 3, 37
Financial Objectives 8
Financial Plan 3, 5, 12, 19, 20, 37, 40
Financial Plan Objectives 38
Financial Planning 3, 11
Financial Planning Process 3, 4
Financial Requirement 7
Financial Resources 4, 7, 44, 107
Financial Strategies 9, 103
   Communicating 9
Financing Capital Expenditure 42
Forecasting 10

Fundamental Adjustments 35
Fundraising 71, 76

G

Generating Income 67
   Investing 74
Grant Claims 45
Grants 42, 68
Growth 30

H

High Morale 90
Human Resource Management 46

I

Income and Expenditure 5
Income Risk 13
Information Management 53
Insurances 19
Interest 70
Internet 55
Intranet 55
Investment Strategies - Long Term 39
Investments 40
   Long Term 41

J

Joint Ventures 43

L

Leasing 43, 56
Legislation 5
Long Term Financial Objectives 30
Long Term Plan 8
Low Morale 90

M

Manageability 35
Management Information Systems 54
Management Strategies 29
Market Testing 107
Materiality 35
Materials Management 57
Maximising Income 67, 117
Minimising Costs 117
Monitoring Activities 11
Monitoring Expenditure 34
Monitoring Process 35
Monitoring Tool 6
More for Less 111

N

Net Expenditure 78
New Service Areas 72

O

Objectives
  Achievable 4
  Realistic 4
Operational Plan 6
Opportunity Cost 89
Outsourcing 107

P

Partnerships 72
Performance Monitoring 52
Performance Plan
  Process. See also *Planning Process*
Personal Aspirations 32
Physical Assets Management 55
Political Risk 14
Politics 31
Present Value 92, 98

Private Finance Initiative (PFI) 43
Private Sector 43, 96
Probabilities 93
Productivity and Unit Costs 52
Profiling 6
Profit 30
Profit Maximisation 30
Public Private Partnerships (PPPs) 43
Public Sector 43, 96
Public Sector Organisations 4
Purchasing 58

Q

Quality 90
Quality Control 58
Quality Standards 39

R

Raising Income 70
Recovery 44
Reducing Risk 92
Rents 69
Reserves 42
Revenue 5, 70
Revenue and Capital Expenditure 10, 13
Revenue Expenditure 39, 43
Risk 41, 74, 89
Risk Analysis 12
  Safety nets 19
Risk Level
  Assessing 15
Risk Reduction 33

S

Scenario Planning 20
Service Plan 6
Service Delivery 96

Service Maximisation 31, 39
Service Risk 13
Service Unit 6
Short Term Plan 8
SMART Objectives 5
Sources of Funds 71
Spare Capacity 75
Specialist Operational Systems 54
Status Quo 32
Stock 58
Strategic Financial Management 35
Strategic Impact 35
Strategy 10

T

Tax Management 46
Tendering 107
Third Parties 73
Time Recording 52
Training and Development 50
Treasury Management 44
TUPE 109

U

Utilising Spare Capacity 75

V

Vacant Posts 49
Vision 5